# THE FIRST THING IS KILL ALL OF THE LAWYERS

JEFFREY MORRISON

Bloomington, IN   Milton Keynes, UK

authorHOUSE™

*AuthorHouse™*
*1663 Liberty Drive, Suite 200*
*Bloomington, IN 47403*
*www.authorhouse.com*
*Phone: 1-800-839-8640*

*AuthorHouse™ UK Ltd.*
*500 Avebury Boulevard*
*Central Milton Keynes, MK9 2BE*
*www.authorhouse.co.uk*
*Phone: 08001974150*

*First published by AuthorHouse 11/27/2006*

*ISBN: 978-1-4259-3630-3 (sc)*

*Printed in the United States of America
Bloomington, Indiana*

*This book is printed on acid-free paper.*

# PROLOGUE

Recently the news alerted the nation that two Duke Lacrosse Players were arrested on a charge of rape. An "exotic" dancer made the accusation that three Duke Lacrosse players raped her during a private party where she and another dancer were performing. In this event, the dancer was described by a security guard in a parking lot later found that she was passed out drunk or in some intoxicated state either drunk from alcohol or in the influence of intoxicating drugs. DNA tests found that there was absolutely no evidence of rape which leads one to conclude that the District Attorney Mike Nifong, had some other motive to file the charges. Mike Nifong had been a lawyer for thirty some years and was the elected District Attorney. As such, he had great power and had perks such as the ability to ignore speed laws and other the like. In addition, the District Attorney was facing an election and refused to allow the potential defendants to allow to surrender to the authorities upon the filing of the charges. The actions of the District Attorney are in unheard of where the potential defendants had secured attorneys and had agreed to surrender promptly upon the charges of filing of any charges. The District Attorney had another motive. It was an attempt to influence the voters, particular black voters to return him to his elected office as District Attorney. Such conduct is outrageous and is a symptom of a power crazed District Attorney. This attorney had just dumped on all of his peers to get an advantage in an election. This is the type of person and many other lawyers that have amassed too much power in their profession, and are those who have lost their way and blinded by their egos. These are the lawyers and all other lawyers that need to be, as Shakespeare said: "kill all the lawyers."

I have just finished reading several books including "Citizen Soldier" by Steven Ambrose and "The Greatest Generation" by Tom Brokaw. These books caused me to recall several stories that I experienced regarding the status of American Justice. While I was in the University of North Carolina, my brother had become a lawyer and was undertaking a general practice in North Carolina. He related a story that illustrates how the legal system has changed from the generation that led us through the Second World War and plunged the American Legal System into a deplorable condition. After beginning practicing law that I had found that the public actually hated lawyers. After several years, it was not difficult to understand why most people in our society have hate lawyers. Most people that have to hire a lawyer were first struck with sticker shock. The initial fee quoted by most lawyers are completely unreasonable. The next problem that people are faced with the problem that the lawyer will not do what the person has hired the lawyer to do. In my own legal situations that I actually had to hire a lawyer to represent me, to file a simple pleading to remove a tenant from my property who refused to pay rent. When I directed the lawyer to file a proceeding to remove the defaulting renter, I was amazed that the lawyer told me that he was not comfortable about filing the proceeding and would not file the dispossessary action. Since I had nearly thirty years in legal practice and considerable practice in landlord law, I was not able to understand that this idiot actually was telling me that he was not comfortable about dispossessing getting a tenant that refused to pay rent. Actually, I really cannot understand any reason why this dummy told me that he was not comfortable about throwing out the non-paying renter.

My brother was representing an individual that was charged with a violation of the North Carolina Controlled Substances Act. The defendant was stopped for speeding. During the stop, the officer decided to search the defendant's vehicle. The officer had no particular reason to search the vehicle, but in those times it was fashionable for the police to attempt to find marijuana. During the search, to which the defendant objected, the officer discovered the suspected illegal contraband. The discovery of the contraband resulted in the criminal charge. The defendant was arrested and jailed. When the District Attorney attempted to offer the contraband into evidence, the defense attorney objected. The objection was raised that the search violated the forth amendment of the American Constitution, which prohibits unreasonable searches without probable cause. If the court ruled that the search violated the fourth amendment of the constitution, then the evidence would be denied into evidence in the trial. If the evidence of the contraband was not admissible into the trial, the charge would have to be dismissed and the defendant discharged and ruled the verdict innocent.

I graduated from the Gambrell School of Law at Emory University. Although I had limited appreciation for my competence, I found that I did fairly well in the pursuit of legal education. I was blessed with the ability of being able to think and decide quickly. During my education I consistently turned in three hour exams in forty-five minutes. At first, my contemporaries thought that I was failing until the grades came out and I scored the best scores in many courses. After I threw my last exam in the box after forty-five minutes in a three-hour exam, I received a standing ovation from my classmates.

In history studies, it is obvious that the American People were steadfastly against the policies of the British that included among things, searches without probable cause. This was one of the reasons that the Bill of Rights was attached to the American Constitution. The judge in the case my brother was handling was confronted by my brother with the argument that the search that produced the contraband was in violation of the fourth amendment of the Constitution. The Judge loudly announced: "Don't give me any of that constitutional hogwash in my courtroom." Thus the lives of all those loyal Americans who fought so valiantly for the freedoms that we are supposed to enjoy were disparaged and callously cast aside by a judge that had no appreciation of liberty. This event has haunted me throughout my career. I have found that this attitude is pervasive throughout the American System. Sometimes the result is driven by the desired result and sometimes it is the result of ignorance. Now, in most cases, the lawyers in our jurisprudence are self ego maniac worthless bags of two hundred pounds of shit in a one hundred fifty pound bags.

One of my fellow classmates called one night and told me that he and his girlfriend had been in an automobile accident. Kenneth was an unusual individual that had an unusual relationship with women. He asked me several about his possibility of recovery in a personal injury claim. The girl was also a lawyer and was the clerk for a well-known judge in the state. I learned that the insurance company said initially that there was no insurance coverage and that they would not pay anything in the injury claim. This seems to have been the attitude of almost insurance claims specialist that I have ever met.

For a lawyer, the desired result in a law suit is achieving the client's desired result. The desired result in a lawsuit is the obvious goal in the practicing of lawyers. At least, in theory, lawyers should attempt to achieve their client's desire. Today, the goals of the lawyers are more apt to try to fatten their wallets. Lawyers today have gotten expert at the delicate surgery known as the wallet-ectomy. In this climate, the potential litigant must try to find a good lawyer, motivate this lawyer to the necessary actions then avoid the pitfalls that may befall the litigant during the duration of the lawsuit. Hopefully, the following anecdotes will assist any potential litigant or anyone who might have to interact with a lawyer. When one wants to achieve a desired result in a legal situation one, must keep in mind what might try to cause the path to veer toward the wrong location. The desired result may be influenced by profit motive or be influenced by cronyism. Sometimes the right result is achieved by an intelligent or imaginative lawyer. When one has absorbed the following situations, hopefully they will be more able to make the correct decisions. It is most difficult as one lawyer might be fabulous in a certain situation but completely worthless in other situations.

I can truly say that I have nothing good to say about insurance companies in situations where the company is the adversary in a personal injury suit. This opinion is derived from the result of not only representing claimants but also from representing insurance companies. Insurance companies go to great lengths to advertise to the public horrible misinformation alleging that juries give away millions of dollars to unworthy claimants. Nothing could be further from the truth. The propaganda campaign carried on by insurance companies had caused the public to believe that (a) there is too far much frivolous litigation and (b) juries give away huge sums to claimants who are fraudulent or at least not nearly as hurt as they have claimed. In most instances this is a terrible tragedy that has been imposed upon the American people. I can say that through my career I have never seen any case in which the claimant got more than they deserved. The television regularly advertise lawyers spouting so-called personal injury lawyers. These personal injury factories must just take and settle the easy cases and never take on difficult cases. When I have represented insurance companies there were many times when we went to the nearest tavern and laughed over a beer or martini about how the jury left the claimant with little or no appreciable recovery. Truthfully, if insurance companies would just offer fair settlements, most people would rather not get a lawyer involved.

When my father in law bought a printing manufacturing company, he found that there were several people that belonged to the union. After he bought the company, he promptly increased salaries and increased benefits. The remaining people in the union dropped their union association. If insurance companies were just so completely dedicated to pinch pennies, most cases would drop their lawyers and settle without lawyers.

At one time, a well-known insurance company revealed that their standard procedure was to initially deny every claim, no matter how valid. Their reasoning that a number of claimants will simply abandon their claims and accept the decision of the insurance company. They do not pursue the matter further. If the claimants get past the first obstacle, the next standard procedure was to refuse to pay until the claimant dragged them kicking and screaming to the courthouse. Years of litigation and delay wear the claimants down and settle with the claimants as cheaply as possible. Insurance companies have no interest accruing during the litigation on the claimants claim. And then, when the Insurance Company has gotten a particularly good lawyer in a case and this lawyer wins a case that never should be won by the Insurance Company, we always suspected that the Insurance Companies executives went to a special room in their office designated as the "laughing room" and laugh for hours laughing about how their great lawyer beat the pants of the poor litigant.

The public really does not know how difficult it is to prepare a case for trial. One must produce sufficient evidence, pay experts, pay deposition charges and then to convince a jury to return a decent award. Usually the judge is sympathetic to the large attorney's firm that usually represents the insurance company. All rulings, in which a court hearing in doubt mainly goes to the favor of the benefit of the insurance company. After all, a judge is a creature of politics and will take the necessary action to promote his self interests. The public never appreciates how badly the deck is stacked against the claimant.

Also, I have seen lawyers that have to ferment litigation in order to keep the litigation going just for their fees. Many divorce lawyers have told their clients that their spouse is getting everything and the only way to save their asses is to litigate. The Personal Injury lawyers regularly have seminars to hone their skills and pass on to each other what tactics are currently are working. At the seminars, claimants learn to never call an incident but rather a "collision". Since the law does not permit the claimant's attorney tell the jury that an insurance company is involved, so the seminars tell the jury panel to ask the jurors if any of them have had any difficulty with "adjusting a claim". After several claims are adjusted, the jury figures out that insurance is involved.

So back to Kenneth and his girlfriend and he had been in an automobile accident. Kenneth asked several questions about the possibility of filing a claim for damage suit. The girl was also a lawyer and was the clerk with a well-known judge. The insurance initially denied that there was any insurance coverage. After the company finally admitted that there was coverage, the insurance company refused to pay any satisfactory amount. Therefore, Kenneth and his girl friend took what they considered necessary action. The girl insisted that Kenneth strike her in her face by Kenneth's fist. This presented Kenneth with a dilemma. He had a psychological dislike of women, but the prospect of hitting a girl frightened him. Eventually he broke down in tears but he hit the girl so hard that her eye was black for months. She applied makeup to accent her eye and they went to the emergency room of the hospital. She went to a medical library to begin research as to what best injury could not be disproved. After settling upon double vision, the girl learned to fake a case of double vision. She persuaded a taxi cab driver to give her a blank receipt book and filled a receipt every day she went to work. She filled receipts for trips for taxi fare to the law library. After about a year, she and Kenneth accumulated a significant amount of medical expenses and expenses for taxi charges. After they put together a viable written documentation that was acceptable to the insurance company. Finally the insurance company relented. In the end she got what she considered a reasonable amount, but certainly more than she deserved.

That is a sorry situation of justice but the insurance companies have made fair settlements unavailable. I recall in the judge's chamber discussing an ongoing case where the lawyer on the other side confessed to the judge that he still has guilt over settling wrongful death cases with uneducated claimants for five hundred dollars or less. Imagine, this company lawyer went into the poor sections of the city and state and sat down at the poor deceased's kitchen table and spread five hundred dollars in cash in twenty or ten dollar bills together with a written release to get the widow to sign and release the insurance company. The widow was tricked to sign away her rights to recovery for the value of her husband's life.

Perhaps it is this background that has led our society to the sorry state we find it in today. In generations past, there was a real sense of honor and dignity between lawyers. One could then rely on a man's word. Today it seems that there is an attitude that has the end justifies the means regardless of cost. In the law profession this has been carried to extremes. The large firm atmosphere requires the young lawyers to bill an impossible amount of eighteen hundred hours to support the extravagant lifestyle. If there was a steroid for lawyers, the young lawyers in large firms would be pumped up the complete fill. When a young associate lawyer hired, he was expected to fill out time slips that total eighteen hundred hours of billable hours per year. When a client sees his bill, he will see hours billed in tenths of hours. Regardless of the amount of time of a telephone call the client is billed at a minimum of .1 hours. If it is a lengthy call, the call will be billed in increments of tenths of hours that probably exceed twice or three times that the actual time. Just to receive a letter, even of a length of one line will be billed at .1 or more.

Within the law firm, there are no ends to the conspiracies. There's a "stab anyone in the back" attitude that permeates the legal structure making it tough for everyone and everything. For the client, I have set down the following that contains a number of situations, both legal and otherwise that when viewed in totals help to understand and navigate in these treacherous waters and protect yourself as a client

Recently, I was asked to consult in the defense of an individual who unfortunately was charged with murder in South Georgia. The trial lawyer had never tried a murder trial and asked for my help. The poor client was Hispanic. During the last years there was a significant influx of immigrants from Georgia from Mexico and other Latin countries. This individual's next unfortunate problem was that he ended up in a small town in South Georgia where there was not exactly abundance of voting Hispanic individuals. His third unfortunate problem was he was involved in a criminal system that operated in South Georgia. Many other jurisdictions have this unfortunate criminal system.

When the Governor of State needs to appoint a judge, they usually look to the prosecutorial offices. Thus, the prosecution attorney's last year will be the next year's judge. Most of the judges are initially appointed from the prosecutors office and then run for judge as the current incumbent. Most lawyers are afraid to oppose them for fear that if they lose, none of their clients will ever get anything close to a fair trial in the future. To lose against an incumbent judge practically can banish a poor lawyer forever from his county of practice and therefore most judges remain judges. Since the judge, being a former prosecutor will still have the same mind that he had when he was a prosecutor. Now both the prosecutor and the judge have the opinion that anyone arrested is guilty. This leaves two prosecutors in every courtroom. All this together, with the fact that the prosecutors have offices in near proximity in the courthouse and rub elbows with the judge every day and you have a system highly slanted in favor of the prosecution.

There is always the outcry that all these accused criminals get tremendous opportunities to escape the charge through loopholes. In real life this almost never happens. A defense lawyer in a criminal case might file fifty motions and probably get about granted none. But the defense lawyers have to resort to trying to find legal loopholes as there is a slim possibility of an accused person getting a fair trial. In reality, the only hope of a fair trial, is when the facts are presented to a jury. The defense lawyer knows that the judge controls what the jury hears and what they do not hear. When the judge is slanted toward conviction, the chances of a real trial are difficult at best. The changes of a fair trail are not good.

The Hispanic young man was living with the victim. He had a son together with the victim. There was a life insurance policy on the life of the victim in the amount of $50,000.00. The testimony was the life insurance was purchased to raise their son in the event of her death. In the murder trial of our young Hispanic man there was no real evidence of his guilt. An intense review of the evidence revealed that there was not a shred of direct evidence of his guilt. The accused had not been anywhere close to the scene of the crime. There were no fingerprints, no eyewitnesses. There was no blood on the accused or his clothing. There were no connections with a murder weapon. The murder scene was splattered with blood and no blood splatter was found on the defendant. When the accused was arrested he was still asleep in his residence and showed no signs of knowledge that a crime had ever been committed. The defendant passed a polygraph examination with flying colors. So how was this man convicted.

Several girlfriends of the victims came into court and testified that the victim had told them that the accused said he was going to kill her and take the enormous proceeds of the life insurance policy victim's life. The appellate court ruled that had ruled about the issue of whether statements such as those made by the victim's girlfriend's could be admissible. Most cases however, such statements were not admissible but in some cases the statements could be admissible. Since there was a possibility that the appellate court might deem admissible the statements, the trial judge allowed the statements.

The District Attorney assigned the case to a female six-month pregnant assistant. A production was made by the prosecutor's contractions. A production was made by the prosecutor's inability to remain standing or be seated too long due to her pregnancy. The victim was beaten to death with wooden coat rack. The judge ruled admissible horrible gory photographs of the victim's autopsy. The judge ruled admissible gory horrible photographs of the murder scene. The judge ruled inadmissible the fact that a known felon who had committed similarly acts in the past had been seen near the vicinity of the murder scene was ruled not admissible. The defendant's lawyer was totally unexperienced in criminal trials. After many hours of deliberations the jury was deadlocked nine to three for conviction. The judge sent the jury back for more deliberations. Finally, the guilty verdict was delivered.

Later the judge felt remorse about the conduct of the trial. The accused, now convicted individual had no more funds to pay for attorneys. The judge called the lead defense trial attorney later and offered to pay for the transcript and offered to cause the county the bill for the attorney to handle the case on appeal. The judge said: "I'll cover you if you want to pad your bill, I just want this man to get a good appeal."

For the public appearances, the judge needed to seem to help the prosecutor. This would help the judge in getting reelected later. He reasoned that the jury would never convict the Hispanic man without any direct evidence. Then after the guilty verdict the judge could not turn over the trial as such publicity would hurt his reelection. Unfortunately, he thought that the appeal would turn over the conviction. Then the judge would seem to the public a law-and-order judge in upcoming elections. The problem with this reasoning was flawed. In order to get rid of bad trial judges, the governor would often kick the ineffective trial judges into the Court of Appeals. By this time, the Court of Appeals was populated with idiots. Forty years ago, an appointment to the Court of Appeals was made as a reward, not as an effort to get rid of a sorry judge. I declined the judge's offer to handle the appeal. I thought that it was better to let someone else straighten this mess. The unfortunate problem for our society is that the real purpose of the discovery of the truth of guilt or innocence with this defendant was really not a factor in the trial.

One of the most unfortunate rulings that I ever had the occasion to witness occurred in a suburb of Atlanta. The Atlanta metro metropolitan area is composed of about six counties. These counties have each own judicial systems. Each have all had quirky rules in the judicial system; some written but some are not. Those who practice in Fulton County, the main county of the City of Atlanta, have a difficult time practicing in other of the nearby outlying counties. This is sometimes referred to as "home cooking." This home cooking gives the lawyers of a particular county a tremendous advantage over a lawyer of other counties. Judge Beggerly was a sitting judge in one of the outlying counties of the metro Atlanta area. When Jimmy Carter was elected president, the democrats went looking to find a candidate to fill a seat of the Federal bench in Atlanta. Some lawyers in a large firm approached Judge Beggerly about whether he would be agreeable about being the Federal Judge. Judge Beggerly was thrilled. Beggerly was not a particularly intelligent person, the only reason that the large firm approached Beggerly was that they considered that he could be controlled. At the same time, other lawyers in the large firm were involved in an important lawsuit that was pending before Judge Beggerly. Beggerly liked the thought of an appointment to a Federal Judgeship where he would never have to run for election as Federal Judges are appointed for life. When the rumor got out, other large firms joined in to promise that they would help Judge Beggerly onto the Federal Bench. All the firms knew that whoever helped Judge Beggerly would be rewarded when they would appear before Judge Beggerly after he got the Federal Judgeship. To demonstrate that how Judge Beggerly could reward those who helped began found that they were given very favorable rulings in Judge Beggerly in his then current courtroom.

In the middle of all of this situation, Jim Nichols went to a bank teller to withdraw some cash. Jim went to a teller and withdrew five hundred dollars in cash in twenty dollar bills. Jim went home and wrote out the payments of his monthly bills. Including of bills was his house payment and in addition, an installment payment on a loan that Jim had for a large tract of land. Jim went out to mail his bills and stopped for a six-pack of beer at the liquor store. When Jim returned home, he noticed that a message on his answering phone. The message requested Jim to call Holly at the bank. Since the bank had closed, Jim did not return the call until the next day. When Jim called the bank and requested the person on the message, he was told that Holly was not in that day and would return on Thursday. Jim asked to have the bank have Holly call Jim whenever she returned. Jim never heard again from Holly at the bank.

The first hint of trouble appeared when Jim's check for his house payment bounced. The next day after the notice of the bounced house payment, Jim received a certified mail letter that notified that Jim's installment loan for the large tract of land had been called due in full and foreclosure proceedings were to be commenced immediately due to the dishonor of Jim's check. Jim went to the bank to find out what had happened. Jim was told that the teller, Holly had not given Jim five hundred dollars but she had given Jim two thousand five hundred dollars. Since Jim did not call back to Holly, she was forced to withdraw the two thousand dollars from Jim's account. Jim protested. When Jim told the bank that he had only taken five hundred in cash from his account. Jim was sternly that the bank security cameras clearly looked like that Jim had gotten two thousand dollars. In addition, Holly's teller drawer was out of balance in the amount of two thousand dollars. Holly remembered that the only person that was given a significant amount of cash was

Jim. When the bank refused to discuss the matter further, Jim went to his lawyer and filed suit against the bank.

Unfortunately, Jim's lawsuit was assigned to Judge Beggerly in the Court of Kangaroo. The bank was represented by the large firm that was promoting Judge Beggerly for Federal Bench so Jim had no chance. After some series initial small discovery proceedings the bank filed a motion for summary judgement. Judge Beggerly promptly granted the motion against Jim ensuring that Jim could not even get his case to the jury. Additionally, Judge Beggerly granted the bank's counterclaim and all tolled Jim owed about $25,000.00. That was the silliest ruling, except for the disaster that befell Jim. Poetic justice did intervene in the end as Jimmy Carter lost the election. Judge Beggerly had resigned his county judgeship in anticipation of the Federal appointment. Jimmy had never gotten to Judge Beggarly's appointment. Then as Judge had alienated all of his county friends and was soundly defeated when Judge tried to get reelected. Again the search for truth was completely ignored by our legal system. No wonder that the public has the opinion that lawyers are worthless.

If Jim had gotten his case to a jury, I am sure that he would have gotten his money back. Juries can make things right. In the case of David Cochran his jury was one of those wonderful occasions where the jury alone made a justice ring. David came into my office with a calamity. David was a house builder specializing in residential houses.

When a developer makes a subdivision, a surveyor is hired to place the lots into the subdivision. The surveyor measures the dimensions of each lot and places pins on each corner. Above these pins are marked with wooden stakes protruding above the ground and tied with bright ribbons. One surveyor was marking in another subdivision and made a small mistake. When he drew the plat, one hundred feet was added to his lot which caused another lot to disappear from the subdivision. When the first builder built the first house, it was situated on lot three but due to the error, the house was actually built on lot four. Then when the builder sold the house, a mortgage was placed on lot three, but the house was really upon lot four. There were several additional houses built before the error so that in all three houses appeared upon the wrong lot and correspondingly the mortgages were similarly wrong. When the surveyor was apprised of the error, he thought that it was not a big deal. The only thing he did was to drop one hundred feet. When it all totaled, there were in excess more than one million dollars of mistakes.

But, at least in this subdivision the lots were accurate. David had selected several lots in a new subdivision in Gwinnett County northeast of Atlanta. David himself located the survey stakes that delineated the lot dimension. He found the front stakes and then found the back stakes. All of the stakes were marked with pink ribbons. From this, he was able to determine the lot dimension and the back, side and front lines. David selected the residential plans for each floor plan and the complete plans for each houses that he intended to build. The first item was to locate the dimensions of the basement for the house that were to be built. He intended to build spec houses. Spec houses are houses that are built for any prospective in the public as opposed to custom houses where the purchaser had already provided the plans to the builder.

Then, David made a mistake. He erroneously located the back points for one particular lot. The lots were arranged in numerical ascending order. When he drew the lots, he used the front points for lot number 3. Unfortunately he used the wrong back points. The lot looked not like a square but more like a parallelogram with about 45 degree angles on the corners. This meant that the lot was skewed such that when he placed the foundation for the house, and tried to place the foundation parallel with the street, the foundation fell about ½ on lot three and ½ on lot four. The correct lot line fell right through the correct divided both lots three and four.

The owner of lot four found about the error nearly immediately. David was blissfully ignorant. As the building of the house on this line between proceeded toward completion, more and more of the construction loan were being paid into the construction. Unfortunately for David, the owner of lot four had contacted a lawyer as soon as David began building on the lot lines. The owner of lot four was aware that David was building over the lot line, but the owner kept quiet. After the house was completed, David was notified by the lawyer by the owner of the problem. Demand was made to David for a staggering amount of money to resolve the error. The owner of lot four demanded that David either move the house and foundation off of lot four, or buy lot four from the owner of lot four at a sum of several hundred thousand of dollars. David was not a wealthy builder and asked for my help.

We refused to accede to the demands of the lot four owner. The lawyer filed suit in the Gwinnett Superior Court where he expected that he would surely be the winner. I pointed to the jury that the plaintiff said nothing and kept in hiding while knowing that David would be building more and more damage. The jury was told that there was way too much litigation in our society and that the plaintiff was really using a dirty trick to trap unsuspecting David. When the case was sent to the jury, I expected that David might be socked with a fifty thousand-dollar judgment. After all, there was no way to get around that there was a complete one half of a house on the lot owner's lot. The jury came back with the verdict. The foreman said that David did not have to pay any money and in addition, David did not have to move the house off of lot four. The courtroom was stunned. I thought it was justice. The lot owner could have stopped David before he built the house to completion. The plaintiff was just too greedy and the jury agreed.

It is really amazing about the facts that jury come with that the lawyers do not think about. Once, in a personal injury case, the plaintiff was crunched when an eighteen-wheeler truck ran over the plaintiff's car. The woman that was driving was claiming terrible injuries. She stayed in the hospital for days and days complaining with headaches. She made the nurses nail sheets over the windows to keep the sunlight out. After the hospital, she complained for years of headaches. The jury was deliberating late into the night. The judge was just about to come back next week to continue the deliberations. The only thing that prevented the trial to continue into the next week was that the water was turned off in the courthouse for street repairs. The judge reasoned that and told the lawyers that after too long, the bathrooms would back up in the jury rooms and the jury would be having to return a verdict. The judge was right. About in one half hour, the jury comes back with a three thousand-dollar verdict for the plaintiff. Why did the plaintiff not get more money? The women on the jury noticed that the plaintiff had her was frosted. If she could stand the procedure of frosting of her hair, she did not believe that she had bad headaches.

No lawyer ever thinks what a jury is going to do. In a motorcycle accident, the jury found clear faults on the part of the defendant. When the jurors tried to agree on an amount, one elder lady refused to agree to any substantial payment. Hours and hours went by with all of the other jurors trying to convince this lady to agree to return a verdict for the injured plaintiff. They started with a sum of one hundred thousand but the lady said absolutely no. Bit by bit the amount went lower and lower but the lady still would not budge. Finally the jurors proposed a sum of ten thousand dollars. Finally the lady relented. She said; " Well, I guess we can give that poor man ten thousand dollars, but it will take a long time for me to get my part saved up to pay for my part of the ten thousand."

After dealing with judges and the legal regular system, and when one cannot either wait for the jury or have the money to pay for a jury trial, there were different ways to go around the system. Charlie chose a different manner to make his money.

When Charlie was in school, he was injured badly in an automobile crash. In his case, the insurance company actually paid a fair settlement, but Charlie was so behind in school that he could not regain his studies until next semester. Charlie took his settlement and paid the money for flying. Charley had a gift for flying. In no time, Charley had gotten his commercial pilot license and just kept flying. Before long, Charley was the main pilot for Panama cargo airlines. After he had several thousand hours of flying, when he had to ground a DC-3 on a mountain top in Georgia. Before the authorities arrived, Charley got lost in the crowd and left. Several years later, Charley was engaged to fly the DC-3 plane off the mountain for a movie called Polk County Pot Plane. The last time anyone had heard from Charley he was touring the country in a van, something about limitations of prosecution.

But the overwhelming better system would be to beat the system and work through the system in imaginative ways. It is always better to settle a case if possible. Such is the manner that was utilized with using Rudy Eudell.

Actually there were two Eudell boys. Both were large in size. These boys were full grown. Both were so large that the only clothes that they could comfortably wear were overalls. Even when Rudy was going to Alaska, he went to a tailor and had a new set of overalls made of cashmere. Rudy could be described as a sloppy person. Every place near him seemed to look as if every thing was thrown on the floor. In the Peanuts cartoon, there was a character called "Pigpen". That would be Rudy except he weighed in excess four hundred pounds. And then, Rudy had a dog, a big dog, a Doberman.

I got a telephone from Sam, another attorney. He knew that I had a good imagination and a good knowledge of real estate. Sam was representing a young woman and described the problem. It seems that an Airline pilot for one of the major airlines had a penchant for young girls. The pilot had found Sam's client when she was twenty years old and the pilot moved her into his house. Later they bought another house and the title was placed in both names, the pilots and the girl. Things were fine for about five years until the pilot decided that the girl was twenty-five and what he really wanted was a twenty old girl. So, he found a new twenty old girl and threw the older girl out of his house. The twenty-five-year-old girl went to my friend Sam, and he called me with the problem.

Normally, the thing to do is to file a lawsuit and ask the court to force the house sold and the proceeds divided. There is a procedure called a partition proceeding. The Court causes the property sold and the proceeds divided between the parties. The only problem with this approach is the time to get a final order especially if the judge actually does the right thing which is never certain. Immediately, I thought about Rudy. I told Sam that what we would do, is to lease the ½ of her portion of her house to Rudy. Then we will move Rudy in with his dog and just live. I figure that we can hitch up a trailer and put in his dog and him in the trailer and back up to the pilot's house. We would open the trailer door and disclose the

Doberman and Rudy that are going to be the pilot's new roommates. It will take too long to Rudy to barge into the bathroom when the new girl is in, and demand to use the toilet immediately. Rudy will sit down and begin, in her presence if she does not actually move enough fast. This should force a settlement in a hurry.

Well when we showed Rudy to the pilot and told him that this is his new roommate, the pilot turned white. We had a bank check in the demanded amount within two hours. Case was won. The only problem is we can't really bill enough as the time needed is too short. Oh well.

The only problem with criminal law is the criminals. How can one ever expect that he can get paid from a criminal? One must remember that the criminal was stealing in the first place. If he had money, he would not need to steal. This makes the practice of criminal law hard to make money. You can't make sure that you will ever get paid, unless you take enough money in the first meeting. Most criminals just don't have that kind of cash. A good friend of mine was a lawyer in Chicago. He related that he had occasionally represented Gypsies. He found quickly that he had to get all of his fee in advance from these people. If not, he said, you will never get another cent. From this situation, one of his associates went into bankruptcy from getting tangled with Gypsies and found that he could not withdraw from the case and could not get any more money from these clients.

And then there is the other thing. Who in the world would ever want to represent some child molester or sexual predators. I can really remember only criminal trial. Before I got out of law school, I began noticing legal cases in the news. One of the first involved particularly stiff sentences that I thought in the case of a school girl in West Georgia who was convicted of taking a $5.00 rocking chair on a house that looked to be vacant. Judge Lamar Knight decided to sentence this girl to the sentence of a jail term of twelve months to be served in the jail. I was dumbfounded that such a sentence could be ruled in this case, so I decided to take action. I wrote a letter to the Governor of Georgia to pardon this girl. In recent order I received a letter that accused me of racism. Jimmy Carter wrote me and said that I must know that the girl is white and I would not write him if the girl was not black and therefore I was a racist. I was so angry that I lost mind and tore up the letter. I now know that such letters would have been great keepsake to be accused a racist by Jimmy Carter, thus demonstrating that Jimmy Carter was an idiot. More and more as I have written this book, I continually see Jimmy Carter make an idiot of himself. It was not surprising that recently, I read a book entitled "The Ten Worst Presidents", I read that the author designated Jimmy Carter as around the top of all the worst presidents in the United States. This author declared that Jimmy Carter demonstrated completely for all the world that the Presidency of the United States was certainly not a job to try to learn on the job. We all remember that the economy was in Carter's presidency. The entire country seemed to be covered by dark malaise. Interest rates had skyrocketed to 21% per annum When Reagan was sworn in as President, the skies cleared and the hostages in Iran were released. Not Jimmy Carter a dismal failure as a President, he was a pig. When we had moved to Georgia, my wife contacted to a classmate from her Collage. The girl worked at the office of the Secretary of State of Georgia. The Secretary at the time was a great gentleman named Ben Fortson. My wife's girlfriend told her to come to the Capitol Building and she would show her she could get a new drivers license in Georgia. At this time the Drivers License office was located in the Capitol Building where the offices of Ben Fortson and the Governor Jimmy Carter were located. My wife found Ben Fortson to be a delightful gentleman, but when she was leaving the Capitol steps she saw Jimmy Carter was coming up the steps. My wife veered left to avoid the Governor, but Carter veered right intentionally to bump into my wife and grope her breast. At those times sexually harassment was not big events, otherwise I would have sued that Carter pig and taken his phoney-baloney Nobel prize and nailed on to my mantle. I was certainly not surprised by Carter's "Lust in his heart " statement. Even now, Jimmy Carter continually nearly daily demonstrates to all that he is an idiot.

I can't remember where I ever found Juanita Hall, but she continued a fixture of my practice at seems forever. I can't even remember how I got into be mixed into her case, but it found me in criminal court representing Juanita Hall striking a criminal jury. This was a first. I didn't even know how to strike a criminal jury.

Juanita Hall was accused of stealing a dollar from the Woolworth lunch counter where she worked. That's right, a dollar, four quarters. The prosecutor would not accept any plea bargains with any reasonable plea bargain. So we went to trial. The judge was old, extremely old, ever for a judge. For two days the trial went on. The judge went to sleep every hour or so and I had to get the bailiff to wake him so I could make an objection. In the testimony that some security officer said that he saw Juanita Hall take the dollar (four quarters) from the cash register. The security officer also testified (by mistake) that he was at about three different locations at one period of time. Obviously he was a liar. Some officers will do any thing to make sure that whomever he thinks is guilty is convicted. Some officers are the worst liars in creation. In the trial I decided to put Juanita on the stand and she was delightful. She called herself over and over: Juanita Hall, which is I. The gallery grew with more people every day. When the jury finally found Juanita innocent, I was treated to a standing ovation. Of course, she has no money to pay me. But, Woolworth had money, so I filed a lawsuit for wrongful prosecution and recovered enough to cover my bill.

It was not really hard to make that security officer make a fool of himself. I knew that he wanted to be a hero. It was evident that he wanted to convict Juanita Hall. It was not difficult to put him in a situation that he was unsure about the conviction. Then he was pushed into making more and more statements to try to make the conviction better for the prosecution. In reality he made it more and more sure that the innocent verdict was correct. By making him try too hard to convict Juanita Hall, it made his testimony more and more incredible. Especially as he put himself in three places at the same time.

In many legal situations, some lawyers tell their clients, that they stay out of danger by saying the same refrain: I cannot recall. Or: I do not remember. I was faced with this tactic in a deposition in a major case against Ford Motor Company. The witness was the President of Ford Motor Company in Europe. We had three lawyers on our side and we were interrogating this witness in Dearborn, Michigan. Several other Ford officials were watching the deposition. In the order of interrogation I was to go last. For four hours with the lawyers on our side, we found that this witness has been coached in this tactic. It seemed that every question was met with the answer: I don't recall. For four hours, I tried to think how in the world that I could get this witness to make meaningful answers. When I was about to begin my portion of questioning, I was struck with an idea. The question I first asked was, Mr. Witness, are you under the influence of alcohol?", next questions I asked were: "Are you under the influence of illegal drugs? , Are you under the influence of prescription drugs? , Are you and alcoholic? , Are you a drug addict? , Are you a mental defective? , Are you suffering brain damage?"I continued in this disparaging line of questioning for another ten minutes or so. When I began into the meat of my interrogation, the witness's memory was remarkably improved

Witnesses can really provide surprises and sometimes fun. My mentor, Jake Cullens had told me several stories to illustrate that fact on several occasions. Jake Cullens was a real original. He was a contemporary of Bobby Lee Cook. Bobby Lee Cook was the inspiration for the TV show "Mattock." Jake tried to avoid the overwhelming notoriety that Bobby Lee Cook got. Jake was the very best. When one looks in the near past in Georgia, and look in the interstate highway system, one finds that three areas that were delayed in finishing. The three areas were in highway 20 near Tom Murphy territory, another area in South Georgia where another personal injury was influential. But the best area was above Marietta in Interstate 75 where Jake Cullens prowled. During the 1960's, Jake made millions of dollars in income in personal verdicts where highway 41 was the required detour where Interstate 75 was unfinished. Jake knew every highway patrolman and policeman in the whole area. Jake gave parties, dove shoots, golf outings all in an attempt to keep the peace officers beholding to Jake. The nineteen hole special events that were legendary. By keeping the police officers happy by golf outing, dove shoots, barbeque and beer together with cash, Jake's police witnesses always told the proper testimony that was most favorable toward Jakes' clients.

Some of Jake's exploits were legendary also. Jake had recovered a judgment against the L & N Railroad for one of Jake's clients. The Railroad was dilatory in paying. After several letters were not responding to Jake for his payment, Jake decided to make sure of his recovery. Sunday, July 4, 1960 at about 2:00PM the Nancy Hanks passengers train stopped in Cartersville. Jake took his judgment and instructed the sheriff to chain the train to the rails. The sheriff went out on the rails and chained the train to the tracts. The sheriff told the engineer that the train could not leave until or unless that Jake's judgment was paid. In about an hour an official of the L & N

Railroad came to the scene. He offered a check in full to Jake to pay the judgment. Jake refused and demanded cash. It was Sunday on July 4 and there was no bank open to get the cash. Jake still demanded cash. The passengers were demanding that the train leave the station. There was no air-conditioned air in the train in those years. After several hours, the bank manager arrived and opened the bank to get the cash for Jake.

After the next month, Jake had a visitor from the railroad. The railroad wanted to hire Jake on a monthly retainer. When Jake asked what, he would need to do for the retainer, the railroad man said that Jake would have to adjust a claim about a cow every month or so but not nothing much. The railroad man showed Jake gold embossed life tickets for Jake and all of his family. Each of their names was stenciled in gold on each ticket. Jake told the railroad that he had just made a fee of about one hundred thousand dollars by suing the railroad last month. Jake declined the retainer. At this time, Jake told me about the chairs in his office. In one of the chairs in his office had been sawed several inches from the front legs. When Jake wanted to get a person out of his office, he demanded that they sit in that chair. From the shortening the front legs, the occupant always felt that he was about to get up and leave.

Every year, Jake put on the Georgia Peace Officers Event at the Georgian Terrace in Atlanta. Any female in that convention that was not working, was thought to be working, and not in registration. Jake hosted several events every year. There was the annual golf tournament that was held near from Jake's home County. After the eighteen hole, the participant was invited to directly go to the nineteenth hole. At the nineteenth hole, the participant found what was essentially a whore house. Then, since this was in Georgia, Jake hosted a dove shoot on the first day of opening day. One of the lawyers that I was in Jake's office went to shoot doves on the next day after Jake's event. He brought back to me a citation for the offense "Hunting on a baited field". He asked me to take care of the ticket. When I asked how he got caught, he told me that several inches of feed were sprayed onto the entire field. The officer had been out of town and had not got the word that the field was Jake's Dove Shoot. It took about 30 seconds to go to Charlie the DA and get the ticket put in the trash can. All of these events were for the Peace Officers in the area. In turn, when there was any automobile collision, the investigating officer would often leave Jake cards with the injured not at fault party in the wreck. Later, the officer would have to testify in the personal injury trial, but they would be sure that he would be paid handsomely for his time in testimony.

Jake told me that one time that he took the Speaker of the House and several Representatives over to the Bahamas to gamble. Jake told me what he had done. He said "Oh No, I just can't believe what I did, Jeff. I actually bribed a customs official to get these women into the United States." That was actually what Jake had done. When Jake came back into the States, he bribed a customs official to allow two ladies into the States with Jake's company. When Jake woke up and sobered up, he found the ladies in his hotel room. Jake looked around and tried to remember what had occurred. When he shook the cobwebs out of his head, he pieced the night in his mind. Jake woke the two women in his hotel room. Jake said: "Ladies, you have three days to gather your belongings to go back."

Well, all testimony during trials did not always work out how Jake intended. It took a small innocent boy who knew how to tell the truth to make Jake's undoing. There was a collision near the Etowah bridge near Highway 41, but a witness of tender years was placed on the stand. During the defendant's attorneys direct questioning of this young boy he got the boy to relate how the wreck actually occurred. It did not go good for Jake's case. In trying to deflect this testimony, Jake interrogated the young boy. It went something like this:

Jake: "Now Larry, do you know who I am? "

Larry: "Yes sir Mr. Cullens, I know who you are.

Jake: "Now Larry, did you really see the wreck exactly how you said? "

Larry "Yes sir Mr. Cullens, It really went just like I said."

Jake: "Now Larry, But you were way all that long way over the mountainside. Wasn't that a long way?

Larry: "Yes, but Mr. Cullens I could see way over there when the wreck occurred."

Jake: "Larry, just how long can you see."

Larry: "Mr. Cullens, I can see the moon."

But some times, and actually more times, the witnesses did just what Jake wanted. During a condemnation case another instance happened. Actually, one of the things that caused the delay of Interstate 75 during Jake's territory was the fact that Jake represented most of the land owners whose land was taken by Eminent Domain. During one trial where a land owner's land was taken, the State's appraiser was testifying in the case. During the direct testimony the State's appraiser told the jury that the land was worth about $200.00 per acre. Jake knew that this was extremely low for the value for the land. When Jake interrogated the appraiser, he started and asked the appraiser if he walked the land. Then Jake asked if the appraiser looked just how the sun set on the mountain site. Then if the appraiser took the feel of the dirt in his hands to see how rich the land was. Then did the appraiser noticed how pretty the rolling hills rolled onto the land. At last, Jake asked: "Don't you think that every foot of the land if worth at least ten cents? " The Appraiser thought, and then said, "Well I guess its worth ten cents? . When multiplied by the square foot of 43,264 feet per acre totals $4,326.40 per acre. That is a lot more than $200.00 per acre, isn't there? It did not take long for the jury to find that the land was worth a whole lot than $200.00 per acre.

Learning from Jake was the most interesting thing that anyone could do. From teaching how to learn a case before a jury, to develop land and to just about anything one could think of, Jake knew how to win. Jake said one could not be a real lawyer until one has been thrown in jail, sued by a client and hauled before a bar with a complaint.

I have always thought that juries were much smarter than most other lawyers think they are. And a lot of times, the jurors are smarter than both of the two lawyers are. I remember one trial in Gwinnett County where I was trying to get a defendant to make him pay for a contract that the defendant signed. It was a simple note. There are just very few defenses against a note that was not paid. I could not believe that the defendant would try to get out of his obligation in this situation, but I guess it takes all kinds. After a two-day trial, the defendant's lawyer went before the jury with a summation where he quoted Latin phrases and tried to confuse the issue. I thought that the people that were selected on this jury were no dummies. My summation began with the following: "You know what you have when you have 100 lawyers on the bottom of the ocean? A good start." My client almost fainted. I continued, " I don't know what a foreign language such as Latin has got with this case, but you guys can read this contract in English. Then I just sat down. It did take not long to get a jury verdict for my client for the amount asked.

Home builders are not really sympathetic defendants. Not many jurors want to side for the builder. Especially if that juror has ever been in a situation where that juror was involved with a builder. I really did not how I got into representing builders. Most lawyers felt that homeowners were usually the winners in the contests. Probably this was the case in overwhelming numbers of actions. Truthfully, most of the time, the builder is the at-fault party. One day Vernon came into my office. Vernon was an unusual individual. He seemed that he should have been a college professor instead of a house builder. He had gotten into a problem with a lawyer who was a notorious entertainment lawyer. Well, Vernon thought that he had finished the house, but the lawyer disagreed. At long last I was able to extract from Vernon from this debacle, but Vernon became a long time client.

The next time that Vernon had gotten into a squabble, it was a much more serious situation. Vernon had contracted to finish a house for an individual that was kind a perfectionist. Well, not kind of a perfectionist, he was a perfectionist. Additionally this homeowner decided to help the builder. Never mind that he had not bought the house yet, but he thought that he was probably going to buy the house and he wanted to assist the builder by adding. It started when the wife wanted to bleed a live chicken over the foundation for luck and the relationship went down from there. I am sure that there were many arguments between the builder and the homeowner. Certainly that I found that Vernon could be difficult. After several months, the relationship finally went to eggs. The last count, it looks that Vernon finally left for the last time leaving about forty thousand dollars unbuilt. The homeowner caused many problems also. Although the homeowner had thousands of wood working tools, he would not assist anything that he perceived that was Vernon's job. When the French doors that went to the backyard were not promptly affixed with door hardware, the owner took handcuffs and secured the doors together.

I am sure that had I any sense that I would not have agreed to represent Vernon, but I did. The trial approached and I tried to settle the case without success. The homeowner had hired a noted firm in Dekalb County and I surely had no power in the County. Nobody had ever heard of my name. The only bright spot was that the Judge was Curtis Tillman, who was a wonderful and honorable person. Judge Tillman came up from the juvenile court. Over the years, I found that Judge Curtis Tillman was the most honorable man in any legal system. Unfortunately, he was very friendly with the defendant's firm for years. Vernon was not particularly a person that I thought would appeal to the jury. But, he was adamant and refused to even think about settlement. You know, the best thing to do, when you think you are going to lose; try to settle. Only take to trial the cases that you think you know that you will win. I was not happy about the situation but there was nothing I could do. Any event, if we were going to lose, I was determined to go down swinging.

The testimony began on Monday. The progress in a trial is that the plaintiff goes first. That means the testimony looks that the plaintiff is going to have the best testimony in the first part of the trial. Usually, your cross examination goes nowhere much. Perry Mason is not going to expose the witness and crack the case at this time. This was not much different. At recesses, the Judge called me in to his chambers and tried to get me to settle the case. Vernon would not even think about it. But when we got into my part of the case, it went better and better. One architect got onto the stand and was really great. He showed how the rough portions never looked great until the finish carpenters got in to cover and caulk and make the house look great. This guy looked over the Judge and showed that the slanted boards above the judge looked that the finish carpenters had not gotten through so that a diagonal board was poised to fall to the Judge. I knew that he was doing well when the Judge had the building maintenance engineers had the board was checked in the lunch recess. Before the trial was finished, I had put into evidence many parts of a house, including a part of a spiral staircase. This court reporter is the poor guy that had to take all of this evidence into his charge. He told that the worst piece of evidence he had to take charge was a live talking parrot that he had to take care for two years. The case was sent to the jury. After about three hours, I heard a cheer from the jury room. Forty-five minutes the jury finally came with a verdict. Vernon had won. The other forty-five minutes to see if the jury wanted to give Vernon some damage for his trouble. About a month later, I got a letter in the mail. To my surprise, one of the jurors had sent me, what only could be described a fan letter. I was described as a Churchill-like orator. I have never gotten over that wonderful event. From that trial, Judge Tillman was a lifelong friend.

Vernon would follow me through the years. He could sometimes be difficult, but he was energetic. The last time, he decided to be his own lawyer. Vernon turned out to be extremely proficient at law. He filed his own case without a lawyer. He thought that he was wronged when he bought five lots in a subdivision in north Fulton. He built his houses but no other builders began building. The developer never built the amenities such as pool, tennis courts, and the like. The developer failed to advertise the subdivision at all when the developer advertised his other subdivisions to great degree. The case progressed and the trial was impending. Actually, the trial was scheduled the next week. Then, Vernon decided that he could not conduct the trial. Vernon called me. Now remember that this case was going for two years with pleadings, discovery and every other thing than the trial and he calls me. He says, Jeff, will you just conduct the trial, I have done every thing else and all you have to do is go to the courthouse. Would you do this? Well, I was an idiot and I said, OK. It takes a lot more than he thinks to get ready to try a case. I have to prepare all of the case arguments that will probably arise into the case, get the jury instructions, and all over things that he has never thought about. Truthfully, when I was in a trial firm, we were taught to be able to go into any trial in such cases, but probably not many other lawyers would try such a venture. In that firm it was usual if one lawyer had a trial date for the upcoming Monday morning for an intersection motor vehicle accident and have asked any other lawyers in the firm to try the case. Only several days were needed to prepare and try the case. But this was unique.

Now, remember that Vernon bought five lots, built five houses, and could not sell them. The bank foreclosed. Just because he could not sell his houses is really the developer's fault, or it? Well, the jury found that the developers were at fault to the tune of Five Hundred Fifty Thousand ($550,000.00) Dollars. Not bad for only one week before I even saw the case.

I never aspired to be a trial attorney. The thought was actually a frightening aspect of law. The how I started was by accident. In law school, I found that I made great grades in Real Property. When I got into the second year, I decided that I might be able to find a real property law firm that would give me a job. That actually worked but I found that to practice real property law was not at all like the study of Real Property law. Soon I was assigned to the deed vault in the dusty courthouse lifting extremely heavy books to "run titles. Other than that, I was a runner. During as which I drove to obscure places in and around Atlanta. The next task was to accomplish any task that was whatever any person did not want to do. Usually these were awful.

One particular time, I remember that the closing attorney asked me to get a signature on a closing statement. In case you do not know what a closing attorney does was to take a pile of papers either supposed by the lender or prepared by his staff and tells the borrower/buyer where to sign on these papers. Often, the borrower becomes agitated, usually as he is asked to pay much more than he expects. In this situation, it is the closing attorney that smooths the problem and attempts to coax the borrower/buyer to part with his cash without bloodshed. In the time where I was asked to get a signature, the borrower had become agitated. In fact, he was downright angry. The borrower had left without signing the closing statement. Of course, I was not told that there was a problem, only to get the signature. I finally found the borrower at his home at dinner. He proceeded to blow all of his anger on me. I will never forget his blew breath from his vegetable soup that blasted on me for a half of an hour. I did get the signature. The import of that signature is that without the papers, the transaction fails and the closing attorney does not get paid. Another duty I had was to pick up the Chinese Food. What happened was the poor owner was able to pay for his divorce and agreed to pay the bill in Chinese take-out. When I started picking up the food, I knew that the firm was getting food about a year. Since there was never a real accounting, the firm just kept on getting food. As much as I know they might still get food from this poor guy. Most often, I was in the "deed room". In every County in Georgia has a vault in the courthouse where the deeds are housed. Most deed rooms are in the basement of the courthouse. The attorneys that search land titles are called "deed dogs. So, I got to know a lot of these deed dogs. This was in the 1970's in Georgia. Land in the early 1970's was beginning to really boom. This was the time of the syndication. Real Property Agents went out on the outside edge of Atlanta and found parcels that had potential. The good agents then talked the farmers into selling and promised that the closing of the transaction in about six months. Thereafter, the agents went out to sell the contract. Groups of individuals that wanted profit would pool their money into a group into a syndication. The agents sold the contracts to the syndications and then the agents told the syndication that the agent could sell the property to another syndication for more profit. This process continued until the contract and the farmer got his land back or the agent actually found an end user that would actually buy the property. Since inflation rates were soaring, the properties kept appreciating and the system kept rolling. During this process, the agent made commissions every time there was a transfer and another closing attorney made to close the transaction. The agents were happy and the attorneys were happy.

Agents bought car phones, new cars, expensive dinners and all of the good life.

Similarly, the closing attorneys raked in the cash. The really good part for the players was they did not to have much cash. The players in a syndication only had to put up their portion of the earnest money to control a significant parcel of land. Typically, only an earnest money deposit of $5,000.00 to $50,000.00 was required to control a million-dollar parcel of land. Since the profit could be expected of maybe 25% on a transaction, a 10% player could put up $500.00 to$5,000.00 on that million dollars to get a return of $25,000.00. It was usual to sell your syndication within three months to get the return. If one was lucky, he could earn $100,000.00 per year from $2,000.00 if he turns four transactions.

The closing attorneys got in the action as did the accountants and the bankers. The 1970's was a flashy age with discos and outrageous bell bottom jeans, Nik-Nik shirts and stupid platform shoes. I went into the house of one of the firm closing attorneys. He showed his closet filled with twenty-five Nik-Nik shirts. The firm worked from eight A.M. until the last closing was complete; sometime as late as 11:00PM. I remember one Friday evening where the poor closing secretary was lying on the floor having a fit trying to figure how to complete the last deal. Surprisingly my extra work did not take from my law school studies. Well, maybe it did, but I did have enough to take other title searches for another attorney. A Timothy was a trial attorney but he supplemented his earnings with syndications. I was asked to search his titles and really found that he and the guys in his firm were real class. I found myself staying more and more around his firm. Soon, I was asked to search the title for the Senior partner in the firm and to complete the closing.

After graduation, after I bounced around, I found joining A Timothy's firm. So, I come in on Thursday and settled into an office. There was nothing particularly going on and I asked A Timothy what to work on. Friday I found a message from another attorney. Bill said, "Please write the application for a writ of certiorari in a particular case. When I find the file, I find that is an Application for a Writ for Certiorari to the United Supreme Court of the United States. After I picked up from the floor, I read further and fell to the ground as the deadline was Monday. Today is Friday. The final draft has to be hand delivered to the printer before 3:00PM. It turns out that one cannot just type a paper to the US Supreme Court. It has to be printed in a certain format in booklet form. Only some handfuls of printers even know the rules how to print the paper. The Application concerns a personal injury when our client is doused with burning air fuel while in his parking lot of his apartment. How I ever got the application in time, but I did and we actually won. I figure that the next weeks of work will not be such dire circumstances, but on Friday, in the firm meeting, the attorney in the Cartersville office got into an argument with the Senior partner. Since the other attorney left the Cartersville office resigned the week before, nobody is left in the office. Monday, I find myself in Cartersville alone. The office was purchased from Jake Cullens and Jake has retired but sometimes came in time to time. At this point, Jake only works as a lobbyist with the Georgia

State Legislature. Rumors still persist that a portion of my duty was to take brown bags filled with fifty bills to be handed out to legislators. Such rumors will still be "classified". The first thing was to review the pending files in the office to find I will have to do. This is the first time that I met Ruben Nunnely.

Nobody knows exactly where Ruben Nunnely came from. He stood about six feet two inches with slicked back red hair. I thought that he must have been called "Red", but I never heard anyone called him Red. Ruben had a lawsuit in the office. He certainly came into the office more than necessary than he needed for his file. He was one of those persons who worshiped Jake. Probably he worked for Jake in some capacity in the past. The court calendars decreed that Ruben would be the first person that I would take to trial in the Cartersville office. The lawsuit revealed that Ruben bought a parcel of property. The parcel was a chicken farm with chickens' houses, chickens feeding equipment and such. I have no idea what one does on at a chicken farm but I guess Ruben did. Ruben paid Twelve Thousand Nine Hundred dollars as a down payment and moved in. A year later, Ruben was gone. It appears that everything not nailed really tight was also gone. All of the chicken feeding equipment and everything a person could carry were gone. Of course all of the chickens were gone. Ruben was distressed. He didn't like the thought that he had lost Twelve Thousand Nine hundred dollars. Ruben had sued to get his money back. This is what I had to ask the jury. Give Ruben's money back to him.

Making the facts worse, there is a principle of law that a felon is regarded not a credible

witness. Ruben was a felon. Ruben was convicted for cattle rustling. Now I had heard of cattle rustling in Texas but this was a new one in Georgia.

When I asked Jake what to do, Jake said: "Just take him to the courthouse and make him a good speech. The secretary said make sure that you prevail. When I said why and she said: "Because losing sucks".

The trial was going to be heard in the Canton Courthouse. The building must have been one hundred fifty years old at that time. The courtroom was the main room in the courthouse. It resembled an auditorium with a balcony, probably where the blacks sat in the old times. During the trial, the elementary second grade came to watch a portion of the trial. The trial lasted three days. It is the only time that I asked if the witness say "didn't he say that he had Ruben like a bull by the tail with on a down hill pull." The bailiff asked if I was old enough to shave. I suspected that several of the jurors knew Jake and two winked at me after one day after the end of the day. Jurors are not supposed to talk with the lawyers other to say hellos or such, but one juror told me to go get them. I had to put Jake on the stand as a witness. It turned out that I was able to prove that the land had a title defect and the jury gave Ruben his money back. This was my beginning into trial practice.

This was not the only chicken rustling case in the north Atlanta area. While discussing my case, a friend in the Cobb County District Attorneys office revealed that he was just assigned a chicken rusting. After a few after hour sessions, he decided to make statements about chicken rustling in the Atlanta area. The defendant was charged with stealing two chickens; certainly not a major crime. However, Sam was not going to let this opportunity go. He refused to plea bargain and demanded that to the defendant that his best offer was two years to serve. This made the defendant's attorney have to go to trial. The defendant's attorney could not believe he was hearing when Sam demanded that the defendant go to jail for ten years. Sam knew the attorney would have to try the case. Even if the defendant lost, no judge would not put the fellow in jail for ten years for two chickens.

Sam was in rare form. He bought a white suit and the kind of black-tie that the Colonel wore. Sam dusted every joke book that he could find that had any chicken jokes. He planned to tell the jury about this fowl deed. How did those two chickens get across the road to the defendant? The poor defendant was simply in the wrong place and time. If the lawyer had any sense, he could have just pled direct to the judge without any agreement from the solicitor. No judge would have given the defendant two years in jail for two chickens. But Sam had bluffed the lawyer into trying the case just to tell jokes. The only other case with more feathers was the computer that failed in the chicken plant feeder. The case was prosecuted by Gary Hatch, defended by Bill Bird and presided by Judge Fryer.

Ruben was a fixture for the next years. Anything I needed, it seemed that Ruben could get done. I would say, "Ruben" and he would reply "Yes'r" It turned out that Ruben somewhat turned out a valuable lesson. I always dictated letters and such and left the tape for the secretary. Since I was not in much of the time, she decided to send my letters without my review. I did mind since I was so busy that it seemed a waste of time until one day. I had dictated a letter about one of Ruben's escapades. At the long letter, I told the other lawyer that he could be accountable in the event he proceeded with a foreclosure without actually getting cash at the time at the action sale. The next day I found that I had not told him that he would be accountable, but rather I said he would be a cannibal. After that, I read all of my letters before they were sent.

In the Cartersville office, I had the opportunity to go through North Georgia. During the travels, I found a wealth of stories. In one county, a lawyer related a story just how damaging circumstantial evidence could be and how this evidence could lead to the wrong appearance. It goes like this: One old farmer went to the barn to check on the livestock. Nature called and the old farmer decided to urinate in the inside the barn. When he was directed his stream with one hand, a sheep bolted toward the open door. The old farmer reached out and grabbed the sheep with its hind leg when his wife walked into the barn. Does the old farmer ever convince that the situation was innocent? "

Then another supposed true was attributed to a local Cartersville attorney named Henry. He was trying a case in where he was the defense lawyer. His client was charged with the heinous crime of seduction. At one time, the seduction of a virtuous woman could be a crime in Georgia. (Now in Georgia, it is no longer a crime but be warned a father may sue for the seduction of his minor when she lives with the parents.) The jury was all male. In those times, in some courthouses had just ladder-back chairs for the jury and no rail between the jurors and the attorneys. This was the situation.    Henry was making his argument. He told the jurors how imagine: 'The night air was cool and clear. There was a gentle breeze. There were you in a carriage all alone. The girl nestled close and snuggled to your side. At that time Henry noticed one juror was very keen about the scene he painted. Henry slapped that juror on the knee and said: "What you would have done, sir? " The old juror jumped to his feet and said, "I would've fucked her is it sent nations to war."

I found that some courthouses had secrets.  In one particular courthouse, one could sit in the last stall in the men's room and overhear what the jury was saying to each other in the jury room. This is a tremendous advantage. If the jury was going the wrong way, just go back and settle your case. In another County, the bailiff was hard of hearing.  Lawyers would loiter near the bailiff when he protected the jury room. Then the lawyer could hear the jurors; the bailiff never figured why he was so popular.

One day in Cartersville a storm appeared in the afternoon just before I was going to go home. The sky turned a strange orange color.  When I got home, I found that an airplane crashed near Cartersville in a town of New Hope, Georgia.   Years later I found myself representing the husband of one of the surviving stewardess.  The stewardess was represented by the firm of F. Lee Bailey. The case was going to trial in the Northern District of Georgia.  This time there would be no jury, just above a Federal Judge. The Defendants were United Airlines, United Technologies, and The Federal Government. The FDA had decided to acknowledge that liability was clear. Therefore, we did not have to prove that the defendant was at fault; just how much they suffered in damages. The damages were fairly certain for the stewardess; she was physically injured in the crash and physiologically damaged from pulling burned bodies and mental trauma. She suffered severe Post Trauma Stress Syndrome. Her psychologist testified as to the horrible mental distress and mental problems she suffered and the fears of flying after the crash. The claims of the husband were less certain. The couple divorced soon after the crash, so the damages amounted companionship for that short time together with certain of the medical expenses. In Georgia, the husband has the responsibility to provide for the medical expenses for the wife. Truly insurance covered most expenses but we were able to waive the claim for the insurance company. Basically, the husband's damages were consortium. This means the husband may recover for injuries to his wife for the loss of her sexual services, society and medical expenses incurred as a consequence to the wife. The judge in our case looked to be about 80 years. We felt that he might not remember how important was the loss of the wife's sexual services. We joked that maybe we could enter evidence of porno films or the dolls that medical doctors use to teach sexual positions. At least the stewardess was pretty; that was a plus.

The trials in Federal were different from I was accustomed in State trials. We started about 10:00AM. The chairs were comfortable swivel rocking leather and overstuffed. We took a thirty minute recess at mid morning. At lunch, we took about one and one-half hours. At mid-afternoon we took another thirty minute break. The trial ended each day at 4:00PM. The Federal Tort Claims Agency sent a hotshot tort defense from the government. The most notable event happened during the testimony of the stewardess. The direct testimony went through all of the horrors of the crash. There were screams, crying, moaning, blood, gore, burning bodies, bodies falling apart from cooking for two hours. At long last, the direct testimony was finished. After all that distressing testimony, we were drained. We took a lunch about two hours to get composed. After lunch, the hotshot lawyer from the Government got to cross examine the stewardess. The first idiot asked was: "Now, what happened when the plane crashed? " I could not believe my ears. For the next two hours were filled with screams, crying, moaning, blood, gore, burning bodies and bodies falling apart from cooking. During the break, one of the other defense attorneys told me: "That stupid son of a bitch. The only thing he could have done worse unless he asked if she knew any thing else she knew that would hurt the defense.~. The stewardess was granted a judgment for high six figures and the husband in the high five figures.

At least I got a good familiarity with the Federal System. Later that would be most helpful. My wife and I lived pretty far outside from Atlanta, at least at that time. Probably it would seem close in. In any event, there were few houses close to us. While she was in her dental hygiene office, she found that another couple of her patients lived near. Ed and his wife lived in a subdivision where there was only one house - his. The amenities had been built so Ed had practically two private tennis courts and a large swimming pool. It turned out that Ed and I were about even in tennis ability - bad, but we began marathon tennis matches. Where we lived there was nothing else to do near. One day Ed came to my house and related a problem. He was so paranoid that he took me into the wooded lot near my house. He was so shook-up that he actually took me into the middle of the woods to make that nobody could overhear what he wanted to tell me. It turned out that Ed had once worked for CW Matthews Contracting Company who built practically all of the roads in Georgia. C. W. Matthews was a powerful and political powerful corporation Ed was a vice president over asphalt manufacturing of the company. When Ed left the company, Ed had bought asphalt machinery and opened an asphalt company near Peachtree City. CW Matthews did take kindly about the competition, so they proceeded to try to run Ed out of business. Matthews would sell asphalt delivered less than Ed could even purchase the ingredients to manufacturing the asphalt. Adding the transportation charges, Matthews was selling much below their costs. In short, unless something could be done, Ed was going down for the count.

Normally, both Federal and State laws prohibit selling products below their costs in an attempt to put a competitor out of business. Many antitrust laws are supposed to protect the "little guys." Ed could file a Federal and/or State lawsuit to try to recoup all of his losses. The only problem is that Ed would have been bankrupt before the suit could get to the suit to the trial. The lawyers for CW Matthews could and would delay the case and bury Ed's lawyers in paperwork, if he could find one willing to take on CW Matthews. Since Ed did not have the money to pay lawyers to take his case, he would have to get a lawyer that would take the case on a contingency fee. When Ed won the case the lawyer would take one third of the recovery plus repay himself all of the expenses that the lawyer had to advance. After the lawyer's fees and expenses, Ed could only get a partial recovery. Then, before Ed could get his money back, his house could be foreclosed and he could be in the poor house.

I took Ed to a law firm that specialized in Antitrust law. While we were discussing all of Ed's relationship with Matthews, we found that Ed was the employee that organized bid rigging in the entire construction industry. This was a huge deal. We found that the entire road construction was riddled with corruption. The money involved was simply staggering. Apparently, Ed would arrange with the major companies such that which project would get and therefore what each company would bid for the State project. Ed was essentially the bag man. This was major information. We could not have found anybody with more information than Ed. When I regained my composure, I sent Ed on to go with the specialized law firm to try to make a deal with CW Matthews. We would tell that if Matthews did not ease off and allow Ed's company to exist in peace, all of the information would be delivered to the Federal Attorney for criminal prosecution.

The big companies are sometime too arrogant. When I went and told the situation to my Uncle in North Carolina, he was not impressed. My Uncle Bob was the President of the biggest company in paving roads in North Carolina. He had a 10% share in this company and has been the President of the company for years. Dickerson, Inc. was essentially the same company in North Carolina as CW Matthews was in Georgia. I told that we had found that Matthews was bid-rigging and that it was seriously criminal and what we proposed to tell Matthews. I was shocked to find that my uncle's company was doing the same thing in North Carolina. I told him that it was illegal and that if this information went to the Federal Prosecutor that there was a substantial chance that his company would be swept into the scandal and he could be in danger in a criminal prosecution. My uncle just laughed. His reply was: "We have always done business this way, we are not going to stop. It has always done this way." When I pleaded with him that it was extremely illegal and he could land in jail, he just laughed. CW Matthews decided that we were either bluffing or not serious or something. The information was described to the Federal Prosecutor's office. The proverbial shit hit the fan. Federal investigations began and the FBI went all over the road construction business. The wheels started rolling. Even though the investigation started slowly at first, soon the investigation began really rolling. As to my uncle, fortunately, he retired before the shit hit the fan. About, twelve months after we had the conversation, and even though my uncle ignored what I said, he retired as he was ever seventy. He obviously did not tell anyone in

Dickerson about our conversation. Later, several major owners of Matthews, Dickerson and others landed in jail for lengthy terms. CW Matthews finally decided that they would leave Ed alone. Ed is prospering even now.

Probably no other aspect of law practice involves more stress than divorce. The parties get crazy. It is a dreadful part of law practice. It does, however, makes for outlandish stories. I really do not why, but it seems that the husband in many cases, must try to control every action of the former wife forever. So emotions are laid bare and tempers are the highest. The strangest things happen in divorce. I really tried to keep away from divorce. The most important fact was that I learned that I never wanted to ever work on one.

It is inevitable that during divorce practice there will be shooting. I came home and heard a client on the answering machine. The client said sometime like this: Please don't file the divorce suit right now. Jerry shot himself." Jerry must not have been a very good shot as he survived. Then later, this same client complained that I did not file the suit soon enough. I did not file the suit as Jerry was still in the hospital and I thought that it would not be very good to have the Sheriff serve Jerry while in his hospital bed.

Jerry was not the only person that could not be good enough shot to kill himself. In one workman man's claim we asked the injured claimant how he was shot. We wanted to know if the injury was related with his work or not. The client said: "Well, I was going to shoot myself in the head, but I didn't and just pointed the gun and shot my leg."

Phil came to see me for domestic advice. It must have been during a period that I was not burned out from divorce and I let my guard down. That's how one gets into the situations. Otherwise, we would run away as fast as we could. I remember that another lawyer that I knew was shot during a divorce case. Fortunately, he had the good sense to trip in a hole in the back yard of his office and the husband thought that he actually hit him and went on to shoot his ex-wife and himself. But anyway, I got tangled with Phil. Phil tells me that his wife is really crazy or crazy or a fox. He relates that he will be peacefully watching television with his kids and his wife will call the police and say that he is beating her. At this time, domestic violence kicks in and all kind of help comes to the wife. The sheriff and deputies summarily throw him out the house with so much as a toothbrush. It takes weeks, psychological counseling and a hearing to get him back into his house. Naturally, he cannot see his kids during this time. After several episodes of this process, Phil decides that he is going to have a divorce. Why is took this long for to Phil to understand, I will never know.

Phil gets nutty. Many husbands get nutty, but Phil is off the edge. He gets obsessed with the thought that his wife is having an affair. If Phil had any sense he would just leave, but Phil gets obsessed. Phil began bringing items to my office to try to prove that she is having an affair. Phil brought plastic bags filled with her underwear. Had I been in the office, I would have thrown his ass immediately out and with his panties. Any event the divorce plods along the way they always go and the property is split and the kids go with the woman and child support is awarded. I think, after all of Phil's effort, the jury gave him one extra percent from the house equity. At least while, we were splitting the property I got to meet Neal Boortz. Later, Neal will talk on his radio show about three days about one of my cases where the husband sends a nude photo of his wife to Gallery Magazine.

When couples are heading for divorce usually, come they are coming to an attorney for the first time. Maybe the spouse had a suspicion or maybe better, they have caught their spouse. One time, the wife suspected that the husband was having an affair, she traveled to their condominium in Destin, Florida. She knew the husband was there and suspected that an affair was afoot. She talked the manager of the complex to allow her to get into the condo. For six hours, she waited in the closet with a camera. When the husband came back to the condo, she remained in the closet. After enough time had passed, or maybe she heard what needed, in the night, she opened the closet door and began flash photos. The startled girl buried into the bed, while the husband tried to explain the naked girl in his bed. The photos were priceless.

Usually, one of the spouses for some reason has to take photos. About once a month I found that an upset spouse brought a set of photos saying, "I can't believe what they are doing on my couch." Better than that, Radio Shack began selling a remarkable gadget. The device enables a recorder placed on the line and turns the recording when the phone is picked up and turned off when the phone is put down. With minimal training, I have the spouse place one of these devices on the house line. The use of this device may be illegal in some states and most states prohibit placing the tapes into evidence, but it surely gets to the truth. Even though the spouse is living in another location, the spouse can usually find an excuse to get into the house for a few minutes to change the tape. Several times, the spouse was talking to their cheating partner while sitting on the very couch that hid the tape recorded beneath them.

And then the spouse can really get mean. The revenge runs to the run of the mill throw away all of his left shoes or cut the left sleeve of his sport coats and suit coats, to really imaginative and brilliant acts of revenge. One husband cut the fuse box out of the house when it was awarded to the wife. He cut enough wire away from the fuse box that the entire electrical system in the house was ruined. To add, he drilled into the floor of the foundation of the house. These holes ruined the waterproofing so the house would flood during any rain. I remember this case well, and believe it after eight years of litigation and dastardly deeds on behalf of the husband, we sat in the Beef & Burgundy Restaurant in Buckhead by the couple who were back together. Normally, the spouse will burn all of his clothes, but one girl went one better. Kathleen took all of Al's underwear and clothes and hung them onto the telephone poles and road signs in their neighborhood. When Al came back from work, he saw all of his clothes hanging.

The sheer most bitter divorce had to be that of Doug's divorce. Doug was brought to me by a private investigator. I say a private investigator. This guy was always in trouble for not having a license as an investigator. Anyway, Doug was one of those husbands that were obsessed with his wife's affairs. Doug had reason to believe that an affair was on going. The wife went jogging with other clothes and never broke a sweat. She went to the grocery, cashed a $200.00 check and bought ten dollars of food. This private investigator had put hours in following the wife and tried to get videotape and even thought that he had a video where the wife was kissing her attorney. The wife had tried to get away from the investigator even high speed chases with the children in the car.

The divorce went from bad to worse to the point that. The wife found from the attorneys advice that she could work the domestic violence system. This left Doug in a meager apartment while she lived in the mansion. Doug drove a Ford Escort while she had the Mercedes. When the domestic ran its course, the wife started into the criminal system. Doug was booked for crimes such as assault and battery. After about three months I got the case to settle down by soothing anger and trying to diffuse the animosity. At one time I had to put up Doug in my house just that Doug could not be accused with another phantom beating. I thought that it was calm so before the weekend that the trial was to commence, I felt good enough to go off for a weekend mini vacation. Of course when I came back, Doug was in jail for attempted murder which made starting the jury trial difficult. Apparently, the wife went into Doug's neighborhood and when Doug went to the store, she was crossing the street and he supposedly tried to run her with Doug's car. A car that small probably wouldn't even cause a bruise, certainly not murder. Doug's wife's attorney had a bunch of photos of the wife's butt that supposedly show a bruise. The only thing anyone could see was her butt.

This divorce would not have been different than everyone's else's except the valuation of Doug's business. Doug had an insurance company and the book of the business had a value could be worth between $100,000.00 and $1,000,000.00. Actually, the animosity was really about the money. All that emotion for nothing but money. Neither party relates surprising different stories from the same event. Doug said that one cold night, and they had run out of wood to burn in their fireplace. There was a piece of furniture that was to be junked so Doug took it apart to burn the wood. The wife said that Doug flew into a rage and smashed the furniture that night. At least, the jury did a decent apportion of the assets. But after this much fighting, there would never be peace between the two. After the trial, Doug died of leukemia. I am sure it was caused by all of the distress and arguing

Love, marriage and money together will result in unexpected circumstances. I have always found that men desire to control any woman that they have ever been married to. Even if the husband has moved on and married another with kids, he often just cannot let go. This happened to a friend of mine when he found the woman he wanted to marry. The woman was a pretty blond that suited Gary perfect. Unfortunately, she had been married before. She had never had children and she had been divorced more than five years.

Her husband caused their breakup when he started with another woman. Later he married the new woman and had several children. But, when he found that his first wife intended to marry another man, he went berserk. He began a terror campaign. Susan would go to her car in the parking lot of the bank where she worked and found nude photographs glued to the door of her car. The photos had been taken by her first husband. In the divorce he agreed to destroy all of the photos that he had of her in comprising poses, however, he reasoned that such did not mean that he would have to destroy the negatives. Other embarrassing things happened to Susan. Her MasterCard for her work purchasers suddenly had charges for porno videotapes. Her locks were filled with super glue, both her car and in her apartment. Gary found nude photos of his fiancee glued to his mailbox and the front door of his house. But the best of all, this creep forged Susan's signature on the model release for Gallery Magazine and sent a nude photo of Susan to Gallery's Beaver Hunt Contest and of course, the photo was printed in the magazine. Next, creep takes several copies of the magazine and places a marker on the page with Susan's photo and takes one copy to Gary, one to Susan's mother and one to the branch of the bank where Susan works. Worst of all, Susan does not get the fifty dollars model fee. Not only that, she does not get the distinctive car decal to place upon her car to advertise that she was a winner in the "Beaver Hunt."

Susan was mortified. She did not want to come to me and have to show the photos to me. Gary and Susan went to some lawyer they did not know. This jack-leg lawyer convinces Gary and Susan to give a release to Gallery Magazine for no money but only to get the model release so they could see what happened. Any idiot should have known to just tell Gallery to give up the model release or they will get a subpoena, but we do not know what the thinking was. Until the case is really messed up, Gary and Susan come to me. After looking this situation, it is going take a lot to straighten out. Obviously, the best suit was against Gallery Magazine. After all, they have money and insurance. But, the magazine has already been released. What needs to be done is to try to avoid the release. If the release holds up, maybe we sue the lawyer that let them off the hook for nothing. If nothing else, the creep may have money; at least we think that his family has money. After we find that we are left with nothing but the suit against creep. Unfortunately, he will not have any money until his mother dies. So, we delay the trial until his mother dies. Fortunately, this strategy works. After we cannot delay the trial anymore, he inherits his mother's money. The next month the jury is selected.

Susan was a nervous wreck. She can't believe that the entire jury will see all of her private photos. I never thought that this trial would attract any notice. Normally, nobody ever watches a civil trial. Maybe some other lawyers that need to be in the courthouse, might look into the courtroom, but never any other persons. Well, this week, a small writer for the local newspaper; I mean local. The next day, the Atlanta papers show up. The third day the radio stations show up and for good measure the TV reporters. The courtroom was completely filled with spectators. That how Neal Boortz picked up on an interview that my wife gave to a radio station. The next three days Boortzs' listeners discuss my wife. To this day my wife and I still wonder was discussed. My wife was on television on noonday a couple days. When the jury comes back with a verdict, the jury takes every penny that creep inherited and gave it to Susan. In addition, Gary gets a verdict, but he mutters to Susan "it is not enough to buy my bass boat.", but Susan assured that she would pitch in. I saw the creep leave the courtroom and vomit in the waste basket. I guess money was great revenge for Susan. My wife knew that the reporters would want to get an interview with Susan. We begged to tell them that when she was asked, "What are you going to do now? " That Susan should say that she is going to Disney world and Gary is going to the Bass Pro Outdoor Store, but she declined. The news of this case was advertised high and wide. The Weekly World News ran a full age on the story. A friend saw the case in USA Today International in Germany and telephoned. I had telephone calls from several TV shows such as "Oprah, but Susan declined. I am glad as all of the shows wanted to have both parties on the show at the same time. It just did not seem the right thing. I had calls from all sorts of naked people with other suits. I did not want to be known as the naked lawyer.

The most unusual aspect of the case was happened to my co-counsel. Mike was a successful trial lawyer and did a darn job of every thing I saw him do. Mike had gone through a divorce and had grown kids. Mike had a pretty girlfriend and I never suspected was amiss. I lost tract of Mike after the nude bank exec. case for several years. About five years later I asked to see if he would like to collaborate on another trial. When I called his office, he seemed the same, but he told me that some things had changed in his life. I thought, "Big Deal." When I went to see him in his office I was not really prepared. It was Mike not that greeted but Andrea. Mike was now Andrea. Mike was a woman. I am sure glad that we never see a nude photo of that one. In any event, I never associated with Mike/Andrea in future cases.

Warner was reputed to have been a CIA agent. In this travels he had extensive contacts in Asia, particularly Korea, Hong Kong, Thailand, and Communist China. A story circulated around that he had swindled a particularly dangerous cartel in Korea and they sent a death squad of ninjas to kill him. Warner simply closed all of his curtains and blinds and stayed in his house out of sight. The ninjas were not about to break in a residence in the US, so after several weeks, the death had spent all of their money. They had to go back to Korea without finishing their mission. Warner was a slippery character. Once he convinced his lawyer that it would be a terrific deal to purchase a train carload of Nike athletic shoes. Nike athletic shoes were about the hottest item going at that time. The shoes were priced way below their cost. Warner neglected to tell his lawyer that all of the shoes were all size twelve. For months this poor lawyer looked every person he saw sizing their feet. In another episode, Warner talked this lawyer into another deal. This time, the lawyer was wary and alert. The merchandise was thoroughly examined and was indeed a great deal. The lawyer secured the merchandise in a guarded in a warehouse and the lawyer kept the only key. Several days later when the lawyer looked in the warehouse, the merchandise was gone. Warner had leased the adjoining building. Unfortunately for the lawyer, there were windows in each place in each of these warehouses. In the dark of the night, Warner some how moved all of the merchandise through the original warehouse into the window of the adjoining warehouse. Warner was just so smooth and likeable no one could prosecute the smiley bastard.

This brings to Jae Ho Han. Warner brought Jae Ho Han to our firm. Friends of Warner in Korea persuaded Warner to find Han to help Han with his company. Most lawyers in Atlanta would not take on a case where Coca Cola was the defendant. After all, Atlanta is the birthplace of Coca-Cola. Coca-Cola has great influence in Atlanta. I figured it would not hurt to at least listen. Han had traveled as the representative of his Korean company to try to talk to a person with Coca-Cola in Atlanta. Han was not successful in getting an audience with officials with Coca-Cola. Han booked himself into a room in a hotel in Atlanta where he was promptly mugged. He lost all of his money, credit cards and his solid gold Rolex watch. When he got to our firm, he was prepared to go to the front door of the main offices of Coca-Cola, douse himself with gasoline and burn himself to death in protest. I persuaded him that it would not hurt the Coca-Cola company for him to burn himself to death in front of their building. Han began to relate the story of the Korean Company, its officials and their plight. It was amazing. It all started with the movie "Star Wars". One of the characters in the movie was a robot named R2D2. Coca-Cola thought that a great marketing ploy to make a radio-controlled toy scalded down model of R2D2 using a Coca-Cola coke can for the body of the robot. Coca-Cola went to toy a manufacturer in Korea. In order to make the dyes to manufacture the toys, the toy manufacturers needed a down payment. Coca-Cola opened an irrevocable letter of credit in a great significant amount so that the Korean banks would forward loans to the toy manufacturers so they could begin tooling up. The Korean toy manufacturers began proceeding with all deliberate speed. At this time, Lucas Films, Ltd. became aware of the project. Lucas Films were the owners of the design patent for R2D2. Lucas Films absolutely refused to license to Coca-Cola the use of the design. This killed the project. Coca-Cola arranged to revoke the irrevocable letters of credit. Normally an irrevocable letter of credit cannot be revoked. Coca-Cola has so much influence and power in the business world that they could revoke the irrevocable letter of credit. The project stopped dead cold. The Korean toy company had already spent hundred thousands of dollars to gear up to manufacture the cobots and then they could not pay their bills.In Korea, unlike in the US, Korean laws protect creditors greatly. When Korean corporations are unable to pay their bills, the officers of the corporation are placed in jail. Han told us the conditions of Korean jails. Han said: "In Korea, jail not nice like in America, In Korea, jail is Monkey cage". Actually, a hole is dug into the ground. The convicted corporate officer is pushed into the hole and the top is secured with bamboo poles. The bamboo

keeps the inmate from climbing out of the hole and has to stay for a sentence of four months. After listening to this horror tale, I was unsure whether I would want to get involved in this case. I conferred with a friend who had done similar cases and struck a deal with him, Andy. I told the Koreans that if they would put up a sum of $40,000.00 for expenses, that Andy and I will take the case. At least I thought that I would get a trip to Korea.

The agreement that Andy and I worked out to divide the work was that one of us would go to Korea and find and interview all of the witnesses and find all of the relevant documents. The other of us would go back to Korea to take the depositions of all the witnesses that we could not bring live to the trial. I wanted originally to go to Korea first. It came about that my schedule prohibited me from going on the first trip to Korea; dammit. Andy went to prepare the case in Korea. He had such a good time from working all day and beautiful women with parties all night in the bath houses and other diversions that he decided that it would not be good for me to go since I was married. Andy went to take all of the depositions along the same work/party format. When the president of the toy company climbed out of the monkey cage, he was so disgusted with the situation that he threw many documents in the trash. Since these documents were crucial, Andy spent days combing the dump to retrieve the documents. Andy worked all day. After every day, Andy was taken out by the clients for Korean beautiful women with night life and bath houses. Andy was so exhausted from the schedule of work and party nights that he got pneumonia. He had to deplane in Hawaii and check into the hospital for several days.

I really wanted to get one of the prototypes of the "cobot." I thought it would be great to drive the toy back and forth around the counsel table during the trial. Sort of a radio controlled a toy coke can, and robot R2D2 look alike. But I never got one of the robots. We settled the case before the case went to trial. The best part was the huge size of the settlement. Unfortunately, a part of the settlement required that no one could divulge the details. I can tell you that my portion was worth nearly a year's salary.

One of the conflicts of my schedule that prevented me from going to Korea was an impending trial date. I guess that if I really wanted to force Andy to send me to Korea for the depositions I could have, but the Fulton Court calendar made it sure that I would not be able to go even if I wanted. A case was going to trial on the schedule in Fulton County. When a case gets in to line it is really difficult to keep from going to trial at the impending court calendar for that month. This particular case began somewhat simply and got progressively more and more involved. My client had originally brought his problem regarding his grandmother's new will. Apparently, his father got her to sign a new will giving everything to him and excluding the grandson. My client related that it was suspicious since granny raised my client and was estranged from my client's father. My client, Jack, said that he thought that granny's signature was not her signature. I kept trying to figure this case out. Now granny did not really own all that much property or money; all that she owned was an old house in Atlanta that she lived with a couple of renters. The renters were disabled former workers that made a party every afternoon of taking prescriptions with codeine and drank copious amounts of beer. But, what are the odds that a son forges his mother's signature on her will to cut off his son from granny's will?

But Jack was adamant that granny's signature was forged and so I employed a questioned document expert to look at the signature. Darned it turns out that the expert says that the signature on the will is not genuine. When we looked further into the circumstances of the signed of the will, it would reveal more suspicious behavior. A young lawyer was hired by Jack's father to write the will for granny. The lawyer never met with Granny, but left the envelope with two renters that lived in granny's house. The young lawyer never talked to the granny before he wrote what she wanted into her will. The fact that the young lawyer failed to talk to his client who wanted the will written was in itself suspicious. Any lawyer should not write a will unless he has talked in person to the person that wanted their will changed. The young lawyer should have been suspicious as soon he was asked to draft a will for an older person that had not met that person who desired the changes in her will. The lawyer was told by granny's son that she wanted to change her will and the son told the young lawyer told what granny wanted in her will. He never even talked to Granny at all.

Then even better or worse depending your perspective, when the renters were questioned, they finally described the suspicious circumstances of the execution of the will. The renters have beer parties every day punctuated with generous amounts of codeine phosphate from pain killers prescribed to the renters for arthritis. They were told by son that granny wanted to sign her new will. The renters took the will into granny's bedroom and helped her trace her signature onto her will. Granny did not even have the ability to sign her own will. The renters had to help her sign her signature onto her will. Although the renters said that granny really had read the new will and granny really wanted to change her will and granny really wanted to try her signature onto the will but she was just too tired to sign without help. The question arose as to why did the young lawyer not met in person with Granny unless there was some question as to   validity.

I was sure that granny had no idea what she had around her for renters and further that she had no idea that the paper placed before her was to be her will.

In Georgia, there are strict requirements surrounding the execution of a will. A lawyer is strongly advisable to be in attendance to make sure that the requirements are followed to ensure properly execution. If the requirements are not strictly followed, the will is not worth the paper it is written upon. My first strategy would be to avoid the will by attacking the execution of the will. To make a proper execution, the person making the will must sign the will in the presence of at least two witnesses and both of these witnesses must sign in the person making the will as well as these other witnesses. When granny is presented with the new will, the two renters are present. We found that granny did not have the strength to sign the will. One of the renters said that granny wanted to sign, but did not have the strength so he helped her to sign the will.

I thought that all the foregoing facts would surely guarantee a win in this case. However, I found out, in an old case decided in Georgia that an assisted signature can be just as good as a normal signature if Granny wanted to sign. Since this is a family quarrel, the case will never settle and I had to forego to trip to Korea and take this case to a jury trial. It turns out that the trial is a real knock down fight from the first to the last. Remember that this estate is not worth probably more than one hundred thousand. The lawyers for Jack's father go so far to hire the best questioned document expert they could find. Actually, this guy had written the textbook on questioned documents. In case anyone wants to know, the expert is Hilton Ordway. Only a person named Hilton Ordway could be the person that wrote the book on questioned documents. Anyway the trial took a whole week. It took a little longer as we had a snow day during the trial. I had left in my car to go to the courthouse, but after forty-five minutes, I had not even gotten out of my subdivision. I asked my wife to call the Judge's home and ask if we were really going to convene the jury trial through the snow. The Judge called back to her and told her to tell me to go on back home and drink some coffee and relax. We could convene the trial the next day if the snow melted. The weather is lousy in Atlanta and I must try a case in Atlanta instead of going to an exotic country. The only time I get a trip to Korea and I am in an old courthouse fighting among family members about an estate less than one hundred thousand dollars. Notwithstanding the

Korean trip, I had been invited to go to the Bahamas. I had high hopes to go to warm Carribean beaches. I had free airplane tickets to leave Friday to go to Nassau. The snow day delayed the trial by one day and caused the trial to continue into Friday. The jury was sent out Friday about 11:00AM. At 4:00PM, I changed the plane tickets later and later as the jurors continued to deliberate later and later. Finally, I changed the tickets to the last plane to Nassau. We finally won the case at about 11:30PM just after the last plane left to Nassau. No Korea and no Nassau.

Saturday night I was not in a nice hotel in a foreign country, but I took my wife to a nice hotel in Atlanta just to get away from our house. At least, we had already arranged to have babysitters and dog sitters so we decided to pretend that we had gone off for a trip. After the weekend, we went to our house in time to go to bed on Sunday night after having a relaxing weekend and looking forward for a good night sleep in our own bed, but at about 3:00AM I got a telephone call from my dentist, Clyde. Apparently, he had left a football game and was nabbed by Atlanta's finest and charged with DUI. Just in case anyone wants to know what to do in this situation, it is to call a bail bondsman. A lawyer really cannot help one much after they have gotten nabbed with an excessive alcohol blood level tested by breath or blood test. Bail bondsmen are experienced in waking at all times of the night where lawyers are not, especially not me. I was trying to look up for a telephone number for a bail bondsman in the phone book when my wife told me that I will never find a bail bondsman in the Playboy magazine. When I finally found the correct book, I told my dentist to call for a bail bond. Call me tomorrow I was going back to sleep.

When I finally got to talk to my dentist the next day, he related an event that had shocked his sensibilities. He had been in his regular routine when two sisters and a brother asked to talk to the dentist. They told Clyde that their momma had fallen and broken a tooth. Momma was in their car in the parking lot. Clyde had a cancellation and told the siblings to bring momma into the waiting room. The siblings told Clyde that they did not think that Clyde really wanted momma in his waiting room due her condition. They said that after Momma had fallen and hit her head, they took her to the hair stylists. Now they wanted Clyde to fix Momma's tooth. A short discussion was had and Clyde finally decided to look at momma in the car. When Clyde opened the car door, he finally realized that momma was dead. Clyde began drinking heavily.

Drunk driving is a serious problem in our country. There are many catastrophes and horrible tragedies caused by drunk drivers. I do not make light of the problem, but we have also seen tragedies that are caused by over zealous prosecutions. The attorneys that defend DUI charges are called DAMM. (Drunk Against Madd Mothers as opposed to Mothers Against Drunk Drivers). I never got into this type of law. It felt too close to criminal law. But when your dentist calls, what can you do?

At one time, defense of cases in Atlanta City was essentially the buddy system. What one did, was to associate the right lawyer that had an association with one of the Atlanta assistant solicitor. The right bottle of a good scotch or the like would bring about the right result. The defendant would plead guilty and pay the fine to the City of Atlanta and then the file of the offense would be thrown into the trash and would never go to the State files. The defendant had no record and no points on his license. That scheme worked well until some over zealous reporter got wind of the fact that this practice was seriously illegal and I believe that some prosecutor attorneys were indicted. However, back then, many locations had similar schemes. In Bartow County, if charged with DUI, the judge would lower the offense to reckless driving if local rule 10 was satisfied. If the lawyer certified to the judge that Rule 10 was satisfied that meant that the defendant had paid a total of $750.00 in fines and attorney fees.

In the time that my dentist had been charged, the buddy was essential gone. The only chance was to get to the Court of Appeals. When one goes to trial in the City of Atlanta Municipal Court, there is not much chance that the judge is going to believe the accused in favor the police officer. The first obstacle is that the judge probably is friendly with the officer or at least knows the officer. Even though the Judge probably knows that the officer is lying through his teeth this fact is probably ignored. Only several Judges such as Andrew Judge Napolitano, who detailed this practice is his book "Constitutional Chaos," do not allow the cops to get away with blatant lying.

I am constantly amazed of the fact that police regularly swear on the bible and then knowingly perjure themselves with impunity. Recently, I went with my sixteen-year-old son who was ticketed due to an outdated license plate on our car. When I looked at the officer's report, I saw another obvious perjury in the testimony. The officer stated that he apprehended my son due to an expired tag that had been expired more than thirty days. The operative "more than thirty days" was the necessary fact that allowed the police officer to stop the vehicle. The vehicle was purchased within two weeks from the stop by the officer. The tag had expired by one day when the officer made the stop. Actually, the tag was a dealer drive-out tag that could not possibly expire more than thirty days. The officer had to lie to make the stop legal. I did not even argue. The officer was trying to find drugs in the car since it was driven by a teenager and was disappointed that he found nothing from his illegal search.

Most of these illegal stops result in many illegal arrests. The judge probably was a former prosecutor and has the opinion that every defendant is guilty. The second obstacle is that the fines the judge levies are going to pay his salary. The judge sees that assistant solicitor every day and knows that each win for the assistant solicitor helps his career. The sum is that your client is going to be convicted.

Back to Clyde's problem, the City of Atlanta Municipal Court does not provide court reporters. If you want one, and you do, you have to pay for and bring your own court reporter. If one does not hire a reporter then one has zero chance of an appeal and the judge and prosecutor can just run over your client with impunity. For my dentist, I had to hire a court reporter. Another oddity about Atlanta Municipal Court is that it starts at 8:00AM. When one lives in the suburbs, one has to get up at 5:00AM to get there on time. Anyway, my dentist is convicted and we go to the Court of Appeals. When you go to the Court of Appeals, the opinion is never announced in court. The Court sends a written opinion in the mail after several months after the hearing. In this case, the Court of Appeals says that the trial judge cannot figure out how or which to believe, the police officer or the defendant. The Court decrees that for all DUI cases, they require that a written statement from the defendant must show that the defendant was offered an independent blood/breath test. This Court Opinion causes a tremendous commotion. This means that since every pending case must be dismissed as no written statement exists. The police must draw up a written "Steed" sheet for every DUI case from the date of my dentist's case. This was my gift to the drunks in Georgia, since the opinion comes out near Christmas. Later, I found that I was the subject of a fan club.

It is surprising how certain police departments get into an investigation. There is a city in Georgia named Kennesaw. This city is the only city in America to my knowledge that has a city ordinance that requires that every head of household must own a gun. Kennesaw is in Cobb County. Cobb County is one of the counties that make up greater Atlanta. Cobb County has birthed several real characters. The local politicians at one time gathered together at happy hour in a local bar in Kennesaw. The bar was located in the "Save-Inn," a motel and bar. One investigation began in one of the rooms in the Save-Inn. When the maids went to clean the room in question, they noticed a significant amount of blood. There were blood spots on the walls, the ceiling, the floor and the bed. The Kennesaw Police began a homicide investigation.

It seemed that a certain judge of Cobb County was one of the politicians that gathered in the Save-Inn bar. One night a woman stumbled into the bar. The patrons said the woman was somewhat scantily dressed and was fairly pretty. Promptly the judge attached himself to the woman and disappeared. The judge kept a room in the Save-Inn for such occurrences and had taken this woman to the room. When the judge heard about the homicide investigation, he called the Kennesaw police. It was reported that the judge said "The Kennesaw police are so stupid that they don't know the difference from a homicide from a good fucking." The investigation quickly was dropped.

Other strange personal injury cases were filed in the Atlanta area. When I was in a defense insurance firm, there were always novel injuries. Once we defended a firm that worked in the airport. The husband of the plaintiff worked as a tram driver. The complaint said that the husband asked to get off time to assist his wife. There was a problem that caused a message not to be delivered promptly to the husband. For some reason after the delivery of the message the husband was not allowed to get time off as quickly as he wanted. The complaint said that since the husband was not able to get home quickly enough, the plaintiff had to give birth at home without assistance. The husband was not able to get off of work in time to get the plaintiff to the hospital. The injury alleged that the plaintiff was sore from the natural birth. This was instantly dubbed the "sore pussy case."

Another injury involved a rear end collision. The plaintiff had been inflicted with whiplash. Probably everyone in America now has heard about whiplash injury. The action of flexion extension of the cervical spine can cause both soft tissue injury and anything up to a broken neck. The condition can cause the vertebra in one's neck damage either to the discs of the spaces or around the soft tissue around the vertebra. It can cause severe pain in a persons's neck and reduce their range of motion in their neck. Motion of the neck can be severely painful. This particularly injury had new issues. This woman alleged in her complaint that the whiplash had rendered her neck so sore that she could not satisfy her boyfriend anymore.

Later a rash of cases came about due to security or lack of security in motels and hotels. One case involved a woman in a local Atlanta motel. The woman was reading a book while reclining on the bed. For some reason she was wearing a negligee and unfortunately the curtains were cracked just enough for someone to look into the room. A rapist broke into the room and repeatedly raped the woman. The plaintiff testified that she was raped over and over. When she was testifying during her deposition, the defense lawyer inquired about the name of the book the woman was reading. The answer was, of course: "Once Is Not Enough."

In late spring in Atlanta, a thunderstorm blew up from the southwest. At this time a young woman was filling her car with gasoline in a Gulf gasoline station near a major intersection. The parking lot of the Gulf Station was illuminated at night by large high sodium pressure lights stationed on the top of large curved poles. When the young woman was walking toward the office to pay for her gasoline, one of the light fixtures fell off of the pole nearest to her and fell onto her head. She was knocked down to the pavement but was soon to get up and seemed fine. But several months later, she lost completely and absolutely the ability to speak and communicate. She could not speak or write. She naturally sued Gulf Oil Company and the owner of the station. This caused a real problem for the insurance lawyers that tried to defend the suit. The lawyers were not able to ask questions or rather they could not get answers from her. This was a perfect case for an unscrupulous claimant. The claimant could not get tripped up with her testimony as she could not talk. In defending the case from the young woman, the lawyers asked the court to allow that she be medically evaluated which was granted but no invasive tests were allowed. This meant that there was not anything that they could not do in reality. Finally, the case was settled for a large sum and I inspected the check to see if the young woman signed her signature on the check. She did not.

Near the time of these cases, I received a call from a client who said that he was hit by a car and was in the hospital. The details were sketchy as he was obviously under the influence of strong pain killers. He requested that I bring a camera over to the hospital tonight to take photographs of his injuries. I was reluctant at first but he insisted that I come to take photographs. I was able to get information that he was on the ground working on his brakes on his own car with his legs protruding out from his car when the other car ran over his thighs. I thought that his injuries would be gory and perhaps that the photos might be necessary to show the jury how bad the injuries were. When I got to the hospital I found his room and prepared to take photographs. When he took the sheets off of his legs, I was amazed to find that there was absolutely nothing wrong with his legs. There was nothing to take photographs of as there was nothing wrong with his legs and his face was ugly. I told him that he had no case and I was upset that he had taken me away from my family for a bogus case. It looked as this was one of those scam artists. At least he did not ask for an advance on his recovery.

I actually had one couple of scam artists that asked for an advance on their recovery. This couple came into my office wearing soft cervical collar on the female claimant. This couple looked as if they had not bathed in a month. They asked that they could smoke in my office I informed that I did not allow smoking in my office. The female then sat in my office and ate the heads off of matches. When they asked for an advance on their prospective recovery, I promptly threw them out of the building.

My friend Bob was a liquor retail store owner. Bob is a big guy. He was special forces ranger in Vietnam. He never talks about much except going to ice cream runs for the officer clubs. But, Bob is more than six feet tall and weighs more than three hundred pounds. Bob is very serious about his stores. Otherwise, is one of the funniest guys in all creation. But, in his store, he is serious. Bob had gotten a ticket for PUI (Pedestrian Under the Influence).

He was actually ticketed for walking drunk. The problem was the aspect of the alcohol in the offense. If Bob got an offense involving alcohol, his liquor license would be revoked. I began negotiating with the assistant solicitor. I could not believe that they were actually serious about prosecuting this charge. After months, I was finally able to talk to the assistant solicitor in to reducing the charge to jaywalking. Just to see if I could get a rise out of Bob, I told him a different story. "Bob. I was able to negotiate out of the alcohol aspect of the charge." Bob said "what happened?" "Well I got the charge reduced to necrophilia with a dog." Bob said "What!" I said, "The good part is that there is no alcohol aspect of the charge but you will probably lose your kids" Bob finally got the joke. Actually the necrophilia charges were some of the animal stories that Bob had told me about his childhood.

Bob was somewhat a juvenile delinquent. One particular neighbor was a serious aggravation to Bob. I don't know remember what this person did to aggravate Bob, but it must have been serious. About ever other day, Bob and his friends would wait after midnight and launch rocks up into the sky and allow the rocks to fall on the poor guy's house. There were so many rocks that the guy was able to build his driveway from rocks. But the rocks kept coming for years, until finally the guy could not stand it anymore. He moved. He moved about forty miles away. Unfortunately, he mistakenly moved to the next door of Bob's best friend. About a week after the guy settled into his new house, the rocks rained again.

The inspiration of the necrophilia charge was Bob's animals stores. He recalled a story from childhood where his family was refused mail delivery at their home. The mailman would always grind up the driveway around their mailbox. As a result a huge mud hole developed in front of the mailbox. Since Bob had the chore to bring the mail every day, Bob was growing more and more mad about the mud hole. Every time Bob would fill the hole, the mailman would grind his tires and throw the gravel out. At least, that was what Bob thought. One day, Bob had gotten just too much. Anticipating the mail delivery about 3:00PM, Bob caught a stray cat in the neighborhood and jammed the cat into the mailbox. This was hot in a summer day in Alabama. When the mailman opened the mailbox to deliver the mail, the cat attacked the mail man with great ferocity. Thereafter, Bob's family was forced to pick up their mail in the post office.

Bob remembered other stories about neighborhood stray pets. One particular dog was the subject of several experiments. One was by taping the dog's feet with bricks and lowering him into the nearby lake to experiment with a scuba dog. After that they tried this dog with a parachute over a cliff, the dog sort of kept away from Bob. After all the animal cruelty stories it seemed that it would be good, to scare Bob because of his actions about the animals.

Bob is paranoid about the possibility that anyone would or could steal from Bob's stores. Bob probably stays 90% of his sleep hours worrying about the possibility that someone could steal anything from him. Once, Bob hired a beautiful woman to test his male cashiers. The woman would dress in a seductive outfit, you know, a skirt so short that she would need two hairdos' to wear and suggest that she really needs a discount. This woman told Bob: "Don't worry, I will get a discount !" When the video security camera and the cash registry receipt demonstrate the illegal discount cause the firing of the former employee immediately. Bob would pay more money and effort to prevent any possibility that a penny would disappear from the "take a penny, leave a penny" bowl. Everyone always said Bob jumped over the dollars to get to the pennies.

In Bob's mind, knowledge of other stores prices are important this his always been Bob's secrets to his success. Bob would not even advertise his prices because he felt that other store owners would find out Bob's prices. Now, Bob would never himself go into another owner's store to "shop" prices. Bob sends his employees into other stores to write others prices down.

About a mile south of one of Bob's stores is another liquor store owned by a Korean gentleman. Bob sent one of his employees to snoop into that store's prices. The next week, the other store's owner came into Bob's store to "shop" Bob's prices. Bob went into a huff. Bob came into his office in an obvious agitated state. Bob's face was red and he looked like a Mexican fighting bull.

Bob said: "Get the hell out of my store. I know that you are not buying. You are just shopping my prices." When the Korean store owner was approached by Bob, the Korean went into a martial arts' stance. Then when Bob picked up the telephone receiver to call the police, the Korean said: "You shop my prices all the time. You motherfucker." The Korean left but Bob was not about to calm down. Bob called me and demanded that a lawsuit be filed.

The best I could think of was to file a civil suit charging slander, assault and trespass. An argument about the charge of slander ensued. The slander was found upon the use of the word motherfucker. We alleged that the use of that word connotes that a public uttering the charge that Bob was said to call a person that had sexual relations with his mother. The defendant charged that the use of the word is nothing but a general derogatory slang. These arguments raged all up to the Court of Appeals, taking Superior Court hearings, appealed to the Court of Appeals, filing of at least twenty page briefs by each side, and a formal oral hearing in the Court of Appeals. For future reference, the Court of Appeals finally decided that the word "motherfucker" actually does not connote sexual conduct.

It is about this time when I got another telephone call in the middle of the night. The connection was poor and there was an echo on the line. I finally figured out that it was Joel Stokes calling from Beijing, China. Stokes and I had been friends for a long time. Joel was rumored to have taken the fall for Andy Young and other black officials in a bank fraud case. Since Joel took the fall he was supposed owed favors. I guessed that this trip to China with Andy Young was some of the payback. Joel had graduated from Brown University and had some football honors in college. Stoke was drafted by the New York Giants after college. Joel told me that he was given a signing bonus of about five thousand dollars which in those times were a great sum. When Joel reported to football camp, he knew that he was going to be a star. He bought a new pair of football shoes just like Jim Brown wore. Joel said that he was going to show that a fast halfback could do well in the NFL.

When Joel went onto the field for the first time, he knew that football would be a great career for him. On the field, Andy Robustelli told Joel that he was going to welcome him to the NFL. Joel went to take the kickoff. The ball came to Joel and started up the field. Joel juked left and then right and woke up on a stretcher on the side of the field. When he looked down, he found his new low topped football shoes on his chest - still tied. That was the last of Joel's football career. He now went into banking.

Joel had the problem that he had a little of larceny in his heart. He always created the most outlandish deals. After he got back from China, he called me and asked me to lease an oil tanker ship. He told me that he knew how to get oil out of Nigeria. Walter Young, Andy Young's brother had done this deal with an oil tanker in Bermuda and made nearly a million dollars. I found out that the actual amount of profit that Walter made was a little more than nine hundred thousand dollars. I had no idea how to lease an oil tanker ship. I told Joel that oil tankers were not job description. Joel was persistent. He would call and tell me that there was a tanker ship in the South Atlantic filled with Nigerian oil and he had all the details. If one had the name of the ship, the name of the captain and the ship's call sign and other documentation of ownership, he could direct the oil wherever he wanted so he could sell the oil.

Joel went on and on about this deal. He said that he went to Nigeria and met with some general. Joel thought that he had a deal with this General. He just had to pirate the oil out of OPEC. At night, the General would give orders to fill Joel's tanker with oil and then Joel would sell the oil while the ship was on the high seas. At one time, Joel wanted me to go to Nigeria with him. He described that the Hyatt Hotel was fenced with razor wire and there was not too much gunfire at night, but we could meet with the General and arrange the Oil deal. I was not about to go to Nigeria for any amount of money or oil. Unlike Walter Young, Joel never got his oil deal.

The next deal involved arbitrage. Joel talked me into going to a meeting at a bar in the Perimeter Marriott. All of the people involved in the arbitrage deals would meet every evening. I had never heard of an arbitrage. Joel and I met with Willa Hayes. Willa Hayes was huge. She was so large that I at first thought that she had been a forward with the Boston Celtics before a sex change. She must have been six feet and six inches tall. I shudder at what she weighed. She was married to a nice man that was about five feet and five inches tall. He could not have weighed more than one hundred thirty pounds soaking wet. It turned out that Willa had a daughter so I guess must not have been a forward player with the Celtics after all.

Willa described the deal that she had almost completed. She had a letter of intent to purchase US Bank Bonds in an amount of ten billion dollars from a European Bank. The interest rate was different from European Banks than the US banks. When the purchase from this tremendous sum, the interest differential would cause a staggering profit. All she needed was a banker from a US bank that would sign a letter of intent to sell the sum of the bonds. It always seemed that the deal was just about to close. In the interim, Willa needed living expenses and money to facilitate to close the deal. There were airplane tickets, hotel room expenses and the like. Willa would reward a person who would assist with the expenses with a portion of the profits.

Willa had reams of paper documenting the deal. There were business cards from bankers from all over around the world. Other people knew some people who finalized some of these deals. At one time, I actually talked to a lawyer in Boston who completed one of these deals. He told me that it took years to finally get a deal closed. He said the girls at First Boston laughed at him for several years before one of these worked. He might have been the only person in the United States that concluded an arbitrage deal. Willa worked years and years. She would find some person who would get the "gold fever" and bankroll her for a while until that person burned out or was broke. Then she would find another financier. I heard the names of probably every major European bank during these deals. There were money deals, bond deals, stock deals, gold deals and oil deals. I did not even know that there was a King Kigali.

When Willa died, I had a telephone call from her daughter. I was just about to hang up on her but I thought it would be too rude and I thought it could not hurt anything. She told me that Willa has succumbed to a kidney infection. She said that Willa had almost finally gotten a gold deal; she just needed more money, but that was not what she was calling about. She finally got to the punch line. "If we cannot pay the bill for the funeral, how long can the funeral parlor keep the body?"

Joel dreamed up the most outlandish schemes, but every now and then he would find something that kept me listening to his ploys. One time, Joel called me and told me that one of his associates needed to talk to me. He said the person just wanted to ask advice and he would pay me five thousand dollars to meet me in a bar and talk. This was too much to pass by so when the individual phoned I arranged to meet with him. I went to Houston's restaurant and bar on Peachtree Street. When we sat down at a booth in the bar, he shoved to me a wad of bills. The bills were so voluminous that I almost could not get them into my pocket. I am sure that I looked strange when I left as I had a decided limp from the cash.

After Joel came back from China, he told me that he had gotten an association with the Chinese main Engineering firm. Supposedly this outfit was one of the world's largest Engineering Company. I was going to go to Mexico for a vacation so Joel decided that I needed to find a parcel of beach that the Chinese could buy and build a resort and golf course. While I was talking to a friend, Dale Briggs, in the bar of the condominiums where I stayed commented that he was looking at a parcel of beach for a golf course and knew the family that owned the three kilometers of beach at Xpu-Ha on the Carribean. Dale had arranged to walk on the property with the owners and asked if I wanted to go along. Dale was going to bring his wife along as they had just gotten back together. Susan and I decided to go also.

When we got to Xpu-Ha, Dale went to the house of the owners to make sure that we were expected. When we got to the beach, we found the most beautiful beach we had ever seen. Dale and Judy wanted to walk north along the beach and we decided to stay. After all, how many times does one have a chance to have a deserted beautiful beach to skinny dip in the Carribean? As we were swimming, we saw a male person walking along the beach. There was no difficulty in seeing that it was a male as he was without clothes and had a penis that fell down to his knees and he waved it toward us. Well we met him later with clothes when he came back to the beach with Dale. Dale, it turns out, knew this character from California. (Dale is a complete book by himself.) After all of this and after copying all of the documents about the property, Joel told us that the Chinese really wanted a beach resort that had ability of gambling. Well, to the next deal.

The last time, I saw Joel he was working on a scheme with World Com before they went bankrupt. Joel had found a contact with World Com and came up with a scheme that would pay Joel and his associates a commission of ten billion dollars. Joel decided that phone cards would be the ticket. If a person joined in the card scheme, the World Com people would fund a scholarship for every person's kids in the club card scheme. All of this was to be sold through all of Joel's civil rights buddies through the neighborhood block captains or such. When I saw letters from World Com agreeing to this plan, I knew that something was amiss with World Com. Sure enough, about a year later, World Com was the largest con scheme since Enron.

Joel was rivaled only with Roger. Roger was a professional plaintiff. He was always falling, slipping tripping, being blown up or such and filing a lawsuit for his injuries. I guess he was selling his body part by part. Thankfully he lived in North Carolina so he could never ask me to represent him. One of the first attempts that Roger tried, he wanted to get rid of his old 1960 thunderbird car. Since he was too lazy to try to sell the car, he wanted to have the car destroyed and file for the insurance claim. He found a place where he could point the car toward the cliff into the river where he could jump out of the car before the car plunged into the river. When Roger got ready, he forgot one thing. When he was guiding the car toward the cliff into the river, he neglected the stop sign. The pole of the stop sign knocked the car door shut and the car plunged over the cliff with Roger in it. He was surprised to find that he was his neck in water. How he got out of the car was a mystery.

Then, since that worked so well, Roger wanted to get rid of another car and for an extra bonus, he would get rid of his brother's car also. During the night, Roger donned his motorcycle helmet, put his seat belt tight, placed two pillows on his steering wheel and crashed head on into his brother's car totaling both cars. Roger was a little banged up so he went to the hospital to get a shot of Demerol. The shot was so good that he went the next night and got another shot. He told me that the insurance adjuster was amazed that Roger hit his brother's car during the accident, but the insurance company paid anyway.

Roger was not only a civil plaintiff, but also he was an expert at working the Workman's Compensation statues in his State. When he was working at a new car dealer, he had the  experience to trip and fall and sprain his ankle. Roger found out that after the doctor put a cast on his leg for a couple of days he was going to be continued his salary. As luck happened, Roger was dating the doctor's nurse and ideas formed in Roger's brain. The first thing he did was to steal a vial of lidocaine from the doctor's office and get a couple of needles for injections. Next, Roger went into his back yard and found a nest of yellow jacket hornets. It was a beautiful summer and the beach beckoned and Roger wanted to go to the beach. After hours, his girlfriend and he went into the doctor's office and cut Roger's cast off. Actually, there was nothing wrong with his ankle. They scheduled Roger with an appointment for two weeks and the nurse was due for a vacation, so they went to the beach as soon as Roger got his paycheck in his mail. They returned two days before the scheduled doctor's appointment. Roger went into his yard and caught several yellow jacked hornets in a jar. Then he injected lidocaine into his leg so he would not feel any pain in his leg and placed the jar opening onto his leg and shook up the hornets. He and his girlfriend went into tho doctor's office that night and put a new cast on Rogers leg and then put a little dirt on the cast to look as it would be a two long cast. The next day, Roger went to his doctor's appointment. The doctor cut the cast of Roger's leg and was aghast. The ankle was sore looking, very red and had much swelling. The doctor was perplexed. The only think thing he could do was to put the cast back for several more weeks. That night, Roger and his girlfriend promptly cut the cast off and Roger went back to the beach. Three weeks later, Roger caught another couple of hornets and injected his leg and repeated the process. Again the doctor was puzzled and the cast went back on, only to be cut off the next night. After about three months, the scam was getting real tired and they were afraid to keep the charade going, but for at least three months, Roger got a paid vacation to the beach.

And in addition, Roger was a gun nut. He had a pistol blow up in his hand and doctored the picture to make him look worse and sued Smith & Wesson to get a brand-new gun. The gun he got was a stainless steel .44 magnum pistol. Roger loaded his own ammunition so he could add just a little extra powder. He also liked to make armor piercing armor bullets. One day he was going to Atlanta when a truck turned into Roger such that Roger was left into the median in the interstate highway. Just to make sure that the trucker was told about it, Roger sped up and shook his fist toward the trucker who promptly knocked Roger back into the median. This really got Roger angry. The trucker was one of those tanker trucks with the stainless tank behind the cab. Roger sped past the truck. Several miles later Roger waited on the trucker with his .44 magnum. When the truck past, Roger shot an armor piercing bullet into the back of the tank. A stream of milk shot out of the tanker. Roger never found out if there was a milk shortage in Atlanta.

The only thing that I helped Roger with was when the Gardner Museum in Boston was robbed of several priceless masterpieces. Roger decided that his uncle had been in on the robbery. There was a reward in the millions. Roger came to see me with his evidence. One of the composite photos of one of the perpetrators looked a lot like Roger's uncle. Roger related that his uncle had done this type of work when he was in the CIA. Roger had talked to his uncle about the exact type of art heist. His uncle had described how he could use a razor knife to cut the painting out of the frames. He told Roger how he would tie the guards with duct tape and spray paint over the security cameras. Roger had gone with his uncle to an art museum in North Carolina where his uncle asked why he couldn't just take one of the paintings. Roger showed how the frame was tied with a security system. When they lifted the frame, the alarm sounded. The guard was told that it was a mistake when he tripped and knocked the frame. Lastly, one of the items taken was a Chinese bronze horse from antiquity. Roger's uncle had a particular penchant for ancient Chinese artifacts. Finally, Roger last saw his uncle with a brand new expensive car soon after the heist. Roger wanted the reward.

The problem was that after Roger told me, there was a real possibility that Roger could be charged with conspiracy and jailed with his uncle. After finding a lawyer in Boston in one of the large firms, I associated that lawyer and we negotiated transactional immunity from the FBI. Then Roger was free to disclose everything that he knew about the heist to the FBI. The robbery has never been solved. Who knows if the uncle had anything to do with the heist, but it surely looked like it.

But the worst episode with Roger was the time that he nearly burned his balls off. Yes, I mean his testicles nearly burned off. One evening Louise and her boyfriend, Tommy had come over to our house to have an evening to play pool and play on some of our pinball machines. Tommy was the harmonica player for the Allman Band which really meant that he was the Allman band drug dealer. Tommy had great stories bout the Allman Brother band such when Greg was in the influence that caused him to be a little paranoid. Greg kept nervously kept looking out of the window worried that someone could look into their window. After about thirty minutes, Tommy finally told Greg Allman emphatically declared that there was no one going to look into their window. After all, they were on the fifteenth story of the hotel.

Anyway while Tommy and Louise were visiting, we got a visit with Roger. Roger had come all of the way from North Carolina to Atlanta to visit and we all thought that we could have a good time playing pinball and playing pool. After several hours, Roger asked if we had any porn tapes that he wanted to try out on his new player. After searching through the closet, we found some old porn VHS tapes for Roger to try out his new player. Roger retired to his room and we all continued to play pool and pinball. After about thirty minutes, someone realized that we had not heard from Roger but we thought nothing it. However after another hour passed and I went to ask Roger if he was alright. I finally got him to come back to our party and we continued with our conversation. After a little time passed, someone realized that Roger had sneaked away and had gone back to his room. Later I went to see if Roger was alright and found him back in front of his porn one man party. This story repeated itself several times until we finally just thought that we would let Roger by himself with his porn party.

The next morning, Roger came to me and confided that he had hurt himself and needed to go to an emergency clinic due to a burn on his genitals. When I told him that I could take him to my friend who was an internist after 1:00PM, Roger told me that the situation was much more pressing and needed immediate care and needed to go to an emergency clinic. It could not wait until 1:00 PM and it was now 9:00AM and Roger wanted to go <u>NOW.</u> To show emphatically how serious the situation was an emergency, Roger opened his bathrobe to reveal skin the color as a red red rose. I was horrified and immediately took Roger to the emergency clinic. Roger insisted that I leave him at the clinic and told me that he would call when he was completed with his treatment. I dutifully left Roger at the clinic and went to work as it was a weekend day and I needed to attend to some pressing business. When Roger called, I was still engaged in my business and called my wife to ask her to retrieve Roger at the emergency clinic. When my wife went to get Roger at the clinic, the emergency doctor pigeon holed my wife and demanded that just exactly what her relationship was with Roger and just what had she done to this man. Roger interceded and told the doctor that my wife had nothing to do with his injuries. Roger's genitals were so burned that one of his testicles were hanging out of its sack. His penis was nearly burned off. The emergency doctor arranged Roger to go to a burn unit in North Carolina and arranged an airplane trip to leave from Atlanta to North Carolina. Then the emergency doctor injected Roger with a whopping amount (about 10 cc's) of morphine and directed me to take Roger to the airport.

After Roger got into the burn unit in the hospital, all of the staff were amazed about the injury. To this point, no one had ever gotten a straight story as to how the injury occurred. Roger stayed in the burn unit for about ten days during the normal treatment. He went forward with such treatments as the debridement and whirlpool treatments. Finally, Roger told me that one day, the skin on his penis got to a state that he was able to roll the skin off of his penis like rolling off a condom. Roger told me that he thought at this point he was good as new. He said it was somewhat being like a virgin. He was ready to start his "new" life - with his great balls of fire.

After the milk shot, Roger did not file a notch in his gun, but we got Diane, a part time judge, to paint a cow on the grip of the pistol. Diane was married to Sam, the chicken rustler prosecutor. Sam also helped when Jay was ticketed with a violation of the Cobb leash law when his dog got loose. Unfortunately, the dog would not stay in the fenced yard. These idiots charged with enforcing the leash laws in this counties, are really unreasonable people. I would not be surprised if the dog officer would not open my yard and when my dog went out of the fence the officer would give me a ticket even if the dog had not even left my yard yet. I always thought that an essential of any crime has to be intent. Such is not the case when dog officers are around. Any way Jay was charged with the leash law. In the interim, the poor dog got out of the fence again and was killed by a car. The animal control officer did not care. By God, he was going to make the case against Jay no matter what. When we found that our friend was the sitting judge that day we decided to have a little fun. We tried to get the animal control officer to dismiss the case since the dog was dead but he refused.

Sam had a tie that had a naked girl on the reverse of the tie. He wore the tie when went into the dog case. We explained that the dog was dead and could not be the subject of any future violation. Then we asked the judge that if he knew the bare facts. At this time, Sam exposed the tie, the judge breaks up laughing and the female clerk dove behind the desk while the officer had no idea what was going on. When everyone got their composure, the judge decided that he would dead docket the case if Jay could ensure that the dog would stay dead. The animal officer was still arguing and had nearly found himself in jail for contempt of court. Later, the female clerk went into the judge's chamber and was telling her friend what had happened that morning. She did not realize that she was swinging her leg while talking on the phone. Her leg was striking the panic button below the judge's desk and several sheriff deputies armed with shotguns broke into the room to defend the judge.

The strangest ticket that I ever saw belonged to a girl that came into my office one day. She brought her ticket with her. When I looked at the charge, I was floored. I had to get into the law books to see if such charge could be charged on a ticket. I found that any criminal charge can be brought by ticket. The girl was charged with sodomy. The Georgia Code defines sodomy as follows:

"16-6-2.

(a) A person commits the offense of sodomy when he of she performs or submits to any sexual act involving the sex organs of one person and the mouth or anus of another. A person commits the offense of aggravated sodomy when he or she commits sodomy with force and against the will of the other person or when he or she commits sodomy with a person who is less than ten years of age. The fact that the person allegedly sodomized is the spouse of a defendant shall not be a defense to a charge of aggravated sodomy."

The girl and her boyfriend were in the back seat of an another friend while resting her head on her boyfriend's lap when a police cruiser came up to the other lane of the street. When the officer looked over to the next car, he saw the girl lying with her head on her boyfriend's lap. I never found out what the result was in the case. The girl had no money and never appeared for the hearing. In such a occurrence, the judge issues a bench warrant for the girl's arrest immediately. Due to the crush of cases in Atlanta, the police do not have the time to look for the girl. Unless the girl gets another ticket or other violation, the police will never look for the girl so at some time the case will expire after a period of time.

Lately, a case load helped Jay avoid a lengthy jail sentence. Jay was jailed for DUI in Atlanta. Jay arranged a bail bond so Jay could be free while the case was working its way through the legal process toward trial. While Jay was on bail and waiting for his trial, Jay was grabbed again for DUI This time, Jay was pulled over at about 8:00AM while he was going to work. Even though Jay had a full night of sleep, the alcohol had not gotten out of his system. Well, Jay went back to his bail bondsman and got out of jail again. Jay did not want to go through the trial. He anticipated that he would be sent to jail at least for a month. Jay did not want to go any time in jail. Jay's doctor decided that Jay could not handle the stress of a trial and could die of the stress on his heart. The doctor certified in writing that Jay could probably die from the stress of the trial. For several years the trial has been waiting for Jay's heart to get better so he can go through the trial. Jay had decided that he was never going to get better.

The only problem was that Jay now does not have a driver's license. Since Jay is a careful driver, he just decided to keep on driving, but only in emergency situations, such to go to the store for cigarettes. Well, Jay had a sailboat in south Florida. When hurricane Ivan was aiming for his boat, Jay had to go to tie his boat better and batten down everything that was loose. When Jay was driving back from Florida, a car next to Jay was speeding which caused the police to pull both cars for speeding. When the Florida State trooper asked for Jay's license, there was none. The trooper searched his computer, he found that Jay's license had been suspended about four years and two DUI charges were pending. The trooper was flabbergasted I thought that the trooper was going to not arrest Jay, but to shoot him.

The trooper had a dilemma. He was due to pick up his son from his first day of school in fifteen minutes. Finally, the trooper told Jay that but for the fact that he had to pick up his kid, Jay would have gone to jail. He gave Jay a ticket for speeding and another ticket for driving for suspended license. He ordered Jay not to drive and left. As soon as the trooper left, Jay drove on. Of course, Jay failed to appear to the tickets in Florida. Had Jay appeared in the Florida courtroom, he would have been sent to jail. Several months later, a letter was sent to Jay. If Jay paid the tickets, the Florida court would be happy. Jay sent a money order to pay for the tickets. Jay had completely avoided the jail possibility.

Jay was the only person that I saw with so many divorces that I considered giving him a group rate of divorces. Before I met him, he had a somewhat successful marriage for eleven years until he got a divorce from Alice. This was the only son he had with any of the marriages. Next, Jay began dating with Candy. Jay and Candy dated for several years and after they met Susan and I they decided to try marriage. Candy was nicked-name Grace, as she either stumbled, tripped, fell, dropped or broke glasses so much that she deserved her nickname. Her other claim to fame was the fact that whenever her name was discussed, every female in the near area would come down with a yeast infection. It was so bad, that any of the female could mention Candy name and get a yeast infection. The Grace name was from the fact that she dropped or broke any glass near her.

Candy and Jay were married before Judge Beggerly. Their marriage lasted at least three weeks. The next time

I saw Judge Beggerly, he remarked that he said: "How did Jay like the slip knot I tied for his marriage?" When one of Candy's mother's friends said, she was upset that their marriage did not last so long. Jay said: "And they said they didn't last!"

Jay found his next wife in his own house. This girl had gotten two DUI charges within three months. There was a problem that one lawyer could not represent both charges at the same time. A lawyer could not represent two charges when one told the judge about any other charge. The only way was for me to represent one charge and that Sam was to represent any other charge. That neither lawyer could know about the other charge when they pled the charge before the judge. The only hope was that if we had both DUI charges and were sent to the same time to the State was that the clerk at the State would confuse both charges were the same and believe that there was only one charge. Unbelievably, the clerk at the State confused the charges and placed only one charge on her record!. We could not actually believe that it worked. Only one DUI charge was lodged onto her record. I have to write that one more time. Only one DUI charge was lodged onto her record.

Anyway, Sam decided that we should go to lunch and congratulate all of us and particularly Cindy about the luck for her. When we went to Friday's restaurant, we happened to be placed in the next booth where Jay's partner was taking lunch with their young receptionist of their company. She was all of eighteen years. Later everyone adjourned to Jay's house where all had drinks only to find that Cindy was dressed with nothing but high heels and pantyhose. Jay fell in love. Cindy immediately moved in Jay's house. She made great strides in learning how to wear spiked heels in Jay's waterbed.

Cindy moved immediately into Jay's house. It did not take much time before there were wedding bells in the air. The ceremony was scheduled for April 1 until Cindy finally figured out that it was an April's fools joke. The ceremony was moved to April 2. This marriage lasted several months. By this time I worked out a group rate for Jay's divorces. Jay went through at least three or four more divorces until he retired.

Close to where Jay lived was a subdivision that Bill Brinson had built. Bill with his partner Martin built hundreds of houses in the Atlanta area. When the Atlanta real estate market was invaded by the boys from California, Brinson and Martin decided to attempt to take advantage of the California boys. Several guys from California got into Brinson and Martin and approached with a proposal. Somehow, they decided to form a syndication where the guys would bring money and Martin and Brinson would find and buy the real estate. The first time they all went to New Orleans to a meeting. They thought that New Orleans was about half for each group to fly. Brinson and Martin went to see how much they could get from the California guys. They brought me just in case. Brinson told me that he did not want to scare the California guys by bringing a lawyer so he told me to stay in the New Orleans Hyatt near the pool bar and they would find me if they needed me. At about two P.M. Brinson found me at the pool bar and brought me several beers and he told me that it was going fine, and for me just to relax at the pool. By six o'clock I was somewhat sunburned and somewhat tipsy when he found me to tell me that everyone was going to dinner. By the end of dinner, the Georgia boys had gotten ten million dollars from the California guys.

Several months later, Brinson was showing the California guys a parcel of land for them to buy. The piece of land looked too good. The price was good; the location was great and the zoning was perfect. When they looked at the land, it just looked perfect so they bought it for their clients in California. What they did not find out, that the land was in the flight path for the Naval Aviation base in Marietta. Brinson had shown the California boys the land when the jets were not going to be flying. When they looked later after they had bought the land, the jet noise was so loud that even at five feet away and shouting at their lungs, they could not hear each other.

When Brinson bought land for his own account he always seemed to find fantastic parcels of land for building. Once while I was with Brinson during the closing, we got to a difficult point in the negotiation. Brinson whispered to me, "Don't argue too much, as I have bulldozers knocking down trees as we speak." The closing went much easier after that revelation.

It took only about twelve months for Brinson to run the California guys out of money. They needed to borrow some money to keep a contract alive and approached one of my partners father-in-law. They got the money but it was well secured and actually in the real estate records in Fulton County reflects that they paid an interest rate of

100% per annum. Then, when they needed an extension, it really got expensive.

Probably the most asked question of clients was "Can they really do that?" The California guys asked that question when they were told what was wanted to get an extension. In divorces, I find that parties ask that question. One husband was ordered to pay child support in what he thought an exorbitant amount. He asked me, "Can the judge make me pay more than I make?" When a particular husband was thrown in jail in Bartow County for refusing child support in the sum of about three thousand dollars. The husband was out of work and told the judge that he had no money to pay child support from. The judge told him that there was no excuse. The husband was dumfounded that he could be put in jail when he really could not pay. The conversation went like this:

Husband: "Judge, I don't understand, I just do not have any money to pay her."

Judge: "That is not an excuse, Bailiff take him away."

Husband: "How much time do I have to serve?"

Judge: "Well, if you don't pay, we will bring you back into court from the jail in six months to see if you have paid yet."

Husband: "What if I can't pay by then?"

Judge: "We put you back in jail for another six months, and so and so - I guess it could turn it into a life sentence."

The husband paid that afternoon.

There are always cases that go all the gamut around the child support and alimony situations. In Georgia, it is weighted in favor for the children, supposedly. There are always some cases when the wife is the bad actor and some when the husband is the bad actor. It seems that one party figures out how to make the law environment work for them. In these cases, one party can really get the shaft.

Years ago, a wife and husband divorced. The husband was an airline pilot. He was a genuine nice man. His wife knew exactly how to set him for long term. She produced a divorcement settlement that she had her attorney to draw up. When the husband was particularly emotionally sensitive, she told him that she just needed the agreement signed. She promised that she would never make him pay the alimony payments. She never tried to ask for payment. She never even talked about the payments. For fifteen years she was completely quiet. When the payments had amassed to a lump sum over one hundred thousand dollars she demanded in full. At this time, the pilot had retired and had no income other than his retirement. The law has changed since somewhat, but at that time, the court allowed her to take 100% of his retirement. There was absolutely nothing that helped him. There was no provision of law that allowed the revision of past due alimony payments. Therefore it was impossible for the pilot to get the sum lowered. The bitch of a wife was not going to help him and since the law allowed 100% of his retirement he was just screwed.

I had a similar case concerning army income. A young divorced wife came to me with the problem that the father would not pay any child support. He divorced the girl and joined the army and was stationed overseas. I finally found him and talked to him to ask about his child support obligations. He told me that he was in Okinawa and there was nothing I could do about it. I told him that I would attempt to attach his income for the back support if he did not pay. He told me to just try. Well, after six months in Okinawa with no income at all, not even cigarettes, he called back. He was irate. He was angry and told me that I should take the back due child support more quickly. I told him that I was taking 100% of his pay now, and the only thing could make it more quickly is if he got a raise.

Lawyers hate to have a client that wants to know what is happening with his case. Usually is due to the fact that the lawyer has not done anything on the client's case. Some clients, however, really behave as pests. The clients begin with the game of "What if". I bought an eight ball fortune teller. Then when the client said "But what if...", I would pick up the eight ball and ask the ball. The answer would appear. The other question is "Can they do that?" The best example of the question was asked by a guy from Turkey. His name was Burnult Gertkce.

Burnult had an antique store. He fell on hard times and he had to file a bankruptcy. When we prepared the papers, we notified all of his creditors. One creditor was the Anatolia Rug Company from New York, NY. After the notices went out to the creditors, the Turk brought a letter to show me. Since I could not read Turkish, I asked what the letter said. He said that the letter says that they say that if the Turk did not pay the amount due to the Anatolia Rug Company, they were going to murder him. The Turk wanted to know if they could really do that if he did not pay. My reply was "Not legally."

One would be amazed that what one can get away with. Once I represented International Paper Company. A lawyer from the main office of International Paper called me about a project that the company had a debt on this project in South Carolina. We devised a scheme how we might get payment for the Company. When the company lawyer came to my office, I told him that the project was in South Carolina about one hundred fifty miles from my office. I had no knowledge of South Carolina law. He replied that he had no knowledge of South Carolina law either, but we figured that we could find the courthouse and research the liens on the project and look up the relevant information in the law library in the courthouse.

We called the nearest private airport and arranged to rent a plane and a pilot. So we got into a Piper single engine four seat airplane and flew to South Carolina. We bounced around at about One hundred miles an hour to a airport near to the county courthouse in South Carolina. We found a taxi and went to the courthouse. When we got tho the courthouse, we found the deed records and looked up all of the liens on the project. We wrote down all of the local lawyers that had filed liens. Then we went to the law library. There is a law library in each of almost every county courthouse in America. We found all of the technical details about how to file liens in South Carolina. We picked a likely suspect and went to the lawyer and told him that his lien was no good, but we would pay him one-third of his claim and would pay him on the spot. When he agreed, there was enough money in the project to get International Paper paid. I picked up five thousand for the afternoon. It remind me how my brother got a person to repay him once. The person wrote a check for my brother knowing that there was not enough in the account to cover the check..My brother found that the check would clear if there was only another twenty dollars in the account so my brother deposited twenty dollars into the account and then cashed the check.

Truthfully, we had no idea if his lien was good or not. It goes to show that sometimes things will work. But, one needs to know how much one can get away without getting in trouble. We represented a group of car dealers. This was a great deal as part of our compensation was driving demonstrator automobiles. That meant that every five thousand miles, I would take my car back to the dealership and pick up a new car and drive the new one. We started with a Ford dealership and then the dealers bought a Chevrolet dealer and then a Lincoln Mercury Jaguar dealership. Just for variety, I would change from a Lincoln Mark Series to a Triumph TR-7.

Back to the lesson as to what one can do without problems. Self help can get one into trouble if one is not careful. The owner of the dealership was an individual named Jim. Jim was an advocate of self help. Even though Jim had our firm on a retainer basis, he found a collector to make sure that debts of the dealership were paid. The collector was a giant of a man named Johnny Graham. Johnny looked like a polar bear with a flat top haircut. He must have been six feet two inches tall and weighed two hundred seventy five pounds. There was no fat on his body. The first time I met him was in Jim's office. I was talking to Jim in his office in the car dealership when Johnny drug in a man dressed in a business suit and handcuffs. The man owed the dealership for a repair bill in the amount of about three hundred dollars. Johnny just broke in the man's office, handcuffed and drug the man into the dealership to pay his bill. I was mortified. My client had just done false arrest, assault and battery together with any number of all sorts of terrible acts. I ran out of Jim's office as fast as I could. But, when I was leaving the dealership I saw a salesman in an altercation with a customer. The customer had cornered the salesman and was seriously threatening the salesman with bodily harm. I interceded and asked what was wrong. The customer said that the salesman had sold him a car and said that the payments would be in a certain amount for thirty-six months. The customer showed us the payment booklet and there were sixty payments coupons in the booklet. At this time, the salesman said: Is that all? I thought that there was a problem. I'll fix this right now." Whereupon the salesman took the payment booklet and threw the last twenty four coupons out of the booklet. That satisfied the customer.

I immediately told Jim that such actions could result in criminal prosecutions and in also civil suits against Jim and the dealership. I did agree that Johnny's actions were effective. Certainly the salesman had defused the customer complaint, but it was not right. Johnny the polar bear with the flat top was still used by Jim for special occasions. Once Ford Credit Company had attempted to repossess an eighteen truck rig from Alabama. When the usual people that Ford Credit had used resulted in the murder of the repo man. The head of Ford Credit asked if Jim knew anyone that could help in this occasion. Jim offered Johnny. Johnny went to Alabama and took the truck. However, Johnny got the wrong truck, so he went back dodged the bullets and repossessed the correct truck.

Jim used Johnny for years for special occasions. Jim was owed ten thousand dollars from an individual in Kentucky and sent Johnny to get the money. The last any one heard from Johnny was during that trip. Johnny called and told Jim that he had obtained the ten thousand dollars in cash. Then Johnny was never heard again. We surmised that Johnny was killed in Kentucky and his body stuffed in an abandoned mine somewhere.

There was always something going around the car dealership. One customer brought a car to the dealer for repairs after a collision. The client told the service manager to dissemble the transmission to see if there was damage in the transmission. When there was no damage in the transmission, the client took the insurance check and cashed it and neglected to pay the dealership. After about ten months, the customer could not figure how to beat out of the dealership for the repair bill. Later the customer to the dealership to try to get something out of the glove box. When he looked at the car, he found that it had been crushed into a box about four feet by six feet.

It is rare to have actual violence in the law business. Threats are common. When trying to collect back child support, I regularly was threatened. I never paid much attention to threats. Usually some irate husband that is required to pay his child support and tells me that he is going to throw a sheet around me and beat me to a pulp. I felt that if some one was really going to do violence, they would not advertise the fact in advance. There were only two times that I paid attention to threats. One time, I was the foreclosure attorney for Countrywide in Georgia. On one loan in North Georgia was noted on the foreclosure package that the borrower was noted for violence. When I caused the foreclosure advertisement in the newspaper I got a telephone call from the borrower. He told me that if I came to the courthouse to commence to auction of the foreclosure I would be shot. There was just something in his voice was so menacing that I was alarmed. North Georgia had a propensity of violence in some parts. I hired Johnny to auction the foreclosure at the courthouse. I told Johnny about the threats, but he just laughed and said: "Do you want me to also throw the borrower in jail in addition to the auction sale?" I just told Johnny that was not necessary, just auction of the property.

Another threat happened when I was alone at home. A voice said "I am going to kill you." I replied, "You must have the wrong number, no one is angry of me." I hung up the phone. The phone rang again. The caller said, "I do not have the wrong number, I coming to get you." I replied, "Well, come on asshole." I promptly loaded my nine millimeter Beretta and my double barreled shotgun. Then I tried to get some sleep. After about thirty minutes, I decided that it was stupid to stay alone in my house. I called Jay and told him what had occurred and asked if I could stay with him at his house tonight. When I got to Jay's house, he and his roommates had donned camo and it looked like an armed camp. It just seemed to be smart rather than worry in my house alone.

Foreclosures in Georgia is a ridiculous ritual. The Lender employs a lawyer to accomplish the act of taking the borrower's house. When the borrower bought his house, he was required to sign a Deed to Secure Debt. This Deed to Secure Debt appoints the Lender as the borrower's attorney at fact so the Lender can sign a deed on behalf for the borrower to whoever person or entity buys the house at a public auction. When the Lender employs the lawyer, the lawyer prepares an advertisement in a newspaper. The newspaper is not the normal paper that most read every day. This newspaper is an obscure paper that only lawyers normally read. Now, the Georgia law requires that the borrower is notified by certified mail. Before too many years, the poor borrower has practically no notice that his house is about to taken from him. No hearing is required before the foreclosure is accomplished. On the first Tuesday of every month, lawyers stand in front of the courthouse and read this silly advertisement in front of usually nobody and sells the house to the lender. No judge needs to allow the lender to take the house. Nobody goes to the borrower before the advertisement. And then his house is sold. No witnesses are needed to show that the lawyer went through the ritual in front of the courthouse. On the first Tuesday of every month between the hours of 10:00AM until 4:00PM one will see a bunch of lawyers in front of the courthouse reading these advertisements. There is no rhyme or reason to the procedure. There can be ten lawyers lined around the steps all talking at the same time. If one tried to find the correct sale it would be exceedingly difficult. Every time that I have had to instruct as to how this procedure is done I find blank stares.

When I told one of my partners, Sheryl, she was dumbfounded. She couldn't believe that she did not have to report the sale to a judge or to the Clerk of the County or someone. Tradition demands that the silly lawyer starts with the phrase "Here Ye, Here Ye". There can be nothing stupider than ten lawyers in front of the courthouse saying at the same time: "Here YE, Here YE". Just to really confound Sheryl, the first time she had to complete a foreclosure, my wife who was in attendance called out: "Sheryl, Did you bring your bell?" It took us three days to convince her that she did not really need a bell to start the sale.

That was even silliest but very more serious. This was the proceeding of that of an attachment action. I filed the attachments numbered 37 and 38 in Gwinnett County, Georgia. An attachment allowed the creditor to seize all of the property of a debtor. The only precondition for an attachment was an affidavit that the debtor either lived out of the state of Georgia or the debtor was trying to hide his assets or attempting to remove the assets out of the state. Our client had a claim against a furniture warehouse store in the approximate amount of $40,000.00. The corporation of the warehouse store was a Delaware corporation, therefore it technically resided out of the state of Georgia. I took three eighteen wheeler trucks, plenty of men and a deputy sheriff and paid a visit to the warehouse. I walked up to the manager of the warehouse and asked for the payment for my client's money. Behind me was the big deputy sheriff with a shotgun. The manager told me that he did not have the money and just what could I do about it. I told him that I had filed an attachment and that if he did not pay right now, I was going to load all of the furniture, take the furniture to a bonded warehouse and sell the furniture in front of the courthouse steps on the next Monday of the next month. The manager's color drained all of his face. He said: "You can't do that!" The deputy sheriff then said: "Boy, I wouldn't be here if this young man could not do just exactly that!" It took almost two days to load all of the furniture and haul it away.

I guess the Lenders figured out that the Lenders would never get their property if the legislature allowed that Judges were required. I have seen some of the lame-brained decisions and reason blubbered out from some Judges.

In a small town in Georgia the Chief of Police was disabled during his duty. The Chief was called upon to go out and arrest a fugitive. The felon was wanted on some heinous charge and the Chief was the only person on duty that was available to arrest the fugitive. The Chief found that the fugitive was home and went to the mobile trailer to arrest the felon. When the Chief tried to place the felon on arrest a struggle ensued. During the fracas, the felon produced a shotgun and tried to shoot the Chief. While the two were struggling with the shotgun, the gun discharged and hit the Chief in his heel on his right foot. The wheels turn slowly sometimes; especially in Civil court. There was a speedy trial and conviction of the felon, however, the felon had a lot of money or property. Normally felons have few precious assets, but in this rare case this felon had money. Since the Chief was not a rich man and had an injury, the Chief decided to sue the felon for his injuries.

The Chief won a jury award in a reasonable amount and went to try to collect the money from the felon. Most people think that after a jury gives out an amount of money the plaintiff gets the money. Wrong ! Only when the defendant has insurance and the insurance company agrees to cover the verdict does the plaintiff  In this case, the felon told the Chief to go to Hell and proceeded to file a Chapter Seven bankruptcy. Now this places the Chief such that if he does not object in the bankruptcy, the felon gets away without paying. The Chief asks for help and we proceeded to see what could done. It turns out that the law suggests that if an intentional act that causes the injury to Chief then the bankruptcy court should order that the felon can not get away without paying. One would think that common sense would allow anyone to figure out that since the felon was resisting arrest, which is an intentional act then having a shotgun going off qualifies as an intentional injury. Unfortunately, the bankruptcy that is assigned to this case is notorious for slowly acting. During the delay, there is a substantial danger that the felon will secrete the money and we will never find it. One would think that a judge would act to assist to a Police Chief. Unfortunately, not this bankruptcy judge. We file the adversity proceeding in the bankruptcy court and the felon and demand a trial. Regardless of what we do the trial is not scheduled until twelve months have elapse. The bankruptcy judge requires a complete trial and then takes all of the testimony and tells that we will hear from him about the ruling. After about six months, the Chief calls to ask what we have heard. Nothing! This judge takes more than eighteen months, that is one and one half years before he writes a ruling. Fortunately he correctly rules that the injury claim cannot be discharged in bankruptcy. Finally we can try to find the felon and try to find his money.

In another judge, the Chief would have had his money in days, not months. The judge can cause the outcome regardless of the facts and law. There is a Georgia law that requires that no person can be convicted of a crime if the person did not intend to break the law. In a great many cases this law is completely disregarded due to financial reasons. Just think if the police had to prove that a speeder had the intent to speed, and prove such intent by a reasonable doubt. Probably there would be a drastic drop in the fines to the municipalities. Years ago, there was a speed trap in a small town in south Georgia. Before the interstate highway system by-passed the town of Ludowici was notorious. It got so bad that when Governor Lester Maddox was the Georgia, he had a billboard erected before the city limits of Ludowici that announced: You are coming near to Ludowici, Don't get stopped in a speed trap, don't get caught in a clip joint." How much is a degree from all out speed traps from the small towns that add to their town budget from setting on the interstate and target speeders.

One warm afternoon in a May, a long suspicious and sinister long black limousine blasted north on I-85 out of Atlanta. After the limousine left the circumstance highway around Atlanta, the car sped up faster and faster. Past Gainesville, Georgia, the limousine was traveling in speeds in excess of one hundred twenty miles per hour. In the next county, the local sheriff's car was stationed in hiding and observing the northbound lanes. The deputy was startled as the black limousine blew by the patrol car. The chase was on. The patrol car was traveling at speeds such that the deputy was afraid to look down to his speed odometer trying to catch the speeder. The chase continued in hot pursuit passed in to South Carolina until finally the patrol caught up to the car and encouraged them to stop. The occupants were bundled into the patrol car and taken back all the way to Franklin County, Georgia. At this time confusion began. The occupants had difficulty understanding English and the deputy and Probate employees could not understand the occupants. Nobody had ever heard the make of the car that the occupants drove. When the Probate Judge of Franklin County arrived, he sized up the situation and called the county attorney. The conversation went much like this:

Probate Judge: "Clem, we got this foreigners and we don't know what to do about them. We found them speeding 120 miles per hour but they keep saying something about diplomatic privilege."

County Attorney, Clem: "Hal, What country do they say they are from?"

Probate Judge: "They say they are from the Soviet Union."

County Attorney: "Have you certified that their passports are genuine?"

Probate Judge: "Yeah, they even say diplomatic on their passports."

County Attorney: "Where do you have them right now?"

Probate Judge: 'I've got them in my office eating square crackers and drinking RC cola."

County Attorney; "Hal, take those boys right back where you found them and tell them you are sorry for bothering them before you start World War III."

Foreign countries can offer some advantages. Romana did not expect to get bad news from the doctor's office, however the news that she heard was devastating. She had gotten throat cancer. Earlier that year, the man that she had lived with for seventeen years had died. Jack had always taken care of her before. Now she felt alone and afraid. Jack had been wealthy but she found that Jack had never gotten around to divorce his former wife. Even after he had never had contact with his former wife, Romana had found out that all of Jack's estate was going to go to his former wife, all seven million dollars. When Romana came to us she didn't know what to do. Neither did we know, however after imaginative thinking we found that in Jack's passport showed that he had gone to Cancun, Mexico about six months before his death. We were dispatched to Cancun for a vacation and scout around when we talked to a Mexican lawyer that I had previous dealings. Perhaps if we looked in the records at the municipal court, there might be a record of where Jack had obtained a divorce when he was in Cancun. The lawyer in Cancun went to the municipal judge and explained the whole situation and described Romana's throat cancer and the other facts surrounding the situation. The judge told us that it would take a lot of time to search through the files for the divorce and it would take him approximately five thousand USD dollars to reimburse for his time. After we paid to the judge five thousand dollars,.the judge went to look into the municipal files for the divorce. This judge had just married Pamela Anderson to Tommy Lee on the beach several months before.

When the judge was looking into the files, we tagged along with this Cancun lawyer to learn some of the Mexican legal practice. We went to the Administration office where needed to dictate a collection suit for one of his clients. The Administration office was right in the middle of the tourist zone where all of the hotels were clustered along the beach. We could look from the Administration office out to the Carribean sea where the sparkling crystal clear waters displayed many colors of blue and green. The Clerk in the Administration office took down his typewriter that looked to be about eighty years old. The typewriter was huge taking all but a corner of the desk. The clerk went into his bottom drawer and took out a piece of carbon paper that had been used many times before and typed the suit as the clerk dictated. As the clerk looked on the clerk's desk, he spied a jar that looked to be pickled artichoke hearts. When he asked the clerk about the jar, we were stunned. The clerk explained that the jar contained fingers. The Judicial Police was interrogating a suspect and got carried away and cut off his fingers. The jar of fingers were evidence. After we caught our breath we left the clerk's office and went to meet the judge to see what he had found. We met the judge in the Pericos, a local establishment.

Surprisingly, the judge found that Jack had indeed obtained a divorce from his former wife and the judge had brought the original divorce decree. Delighted we enjoyed the surroundings of Cancun and left back to Atlanta several days later.

After we disclosed the former wife's attorney caused a substantial uproar. The wife's supposed seven million dollars inheritance had disappeared. Several weeks later we got a call from Cancun and we were needed to come back to assist to final the divorce decree. The wife's lawyer had obtained a Mexican lawyer and there was a conflict with our lawyer and her lawyer which unknown to each other had each taken sides against each other. The Partnership in the Cancun had made a mistake. One partner represented us and his partner had undertook to represent the former wife. When they found this out they did not know what to do. The capital of the State of Quintana Roo in which Cancun is located is the city of Chetemal. We had to dispatch to go to Chetemal and look into the official records to document if the judge had sent the divorce decree for final documentation. Fortunately the case was settled before it went much father. Even if the judge had not documented the decree in the files in

Chetemal, he could have added in the marginal notes but it might have been a sticky situation.

One day in Dog court, I listened to the testimony of one particular case. The evidence that a defendant was ticketed with a violation of the leash law that required that a dog be on a leash when not fenced. The testimony was that a painter had accidentally left the fence open. The homeowner came home to find the dog officer ready to ticket him.

"Georgia Code 16-2-2.

A person shall not be found guilty of any crime committed by misfortune or accident where it satisfactorily appears that there was no criminal scheme or undertaking, intention or criminal negligence." The homeowner was found guilty.The only way to convict the homeowner is for the judge to disregard the plain law. The judge must reason that the county needs the revenue from the fines or there is some policy that demands we lock our pets to such degree to demand strict compliance or the judge needs to assist the police officer. Somewhere the legal system has gone wrong. I hope that after reading all of this legal true situations, you can find imaginative actions so you can avoid this system.

The problem with the legal system as it exists now, it that the people that wave gotten into the Bar Association and find that the legal profession is populated with larger and larger firms. There are megaliths of numbers that number thousands of lawyers. The only way to make this profitable and remunerate the bigger partners demands that the profession must be controlled by these megaliths.

To that end, these firms drive out all competition. As a result, the fees have risen markedly. Where a senior partner might bill at the rate of $140.00 per hour, these same persons are billing at a rate of a thousand dollars per hour and more.

These large firms target the sole practitioner by every mean. Especially when the firm detects a gifted sole practitioner at every turn, the sole practitioner is attacked. His clients are stolen and firm himself targeted by bar complaints and malpractice suits. The other tragedy is when these bar complaints come to the bar association, the sole practitioner finds judged by members of large firms. The large have the ability to vote their members into the governing board of the bar associations. As a result, there is no real chance for the sole practitioner. More and more the large firms are strangling the smaller firms. As for the general population, their legal representation has gone exorbitant as the large firms get more and more monopolistic tactics. Now the only real hope for the general population is to first kill all the lawyers.

# About the Author

Jeffrey Morrison was born in Salisbury, North Carolina May 1, 1949. He graduated from The University of North Carolina at Chapel Hill. During the university he played in a rock & roll bands. He married Susan Reed Hardesty in August 1971 and went to law school at Emory University. For more than twenty years he practiced law in Atlanta, Georgia until he went to other honorable professions. Today he is in the process of moving to Belize, Central America.